Living Reiki

Takata's Teachings

as told to

Fran Brown

LifeRhythm

Many thanks to Gunter Baylow
for permission to use the cover photograph.

Library of Congress Cataloging-in-Publication Data

Brown, Fran, 1924-
Living Reiki : Takata's teachings / Fran Brown
ISBN 0-940795-10-8
1. Reiki (Healing system) 2. Takata, Hawayo Kawamuri, 1900-1980.
3. Healers--Hawaii--Biography I. Title
RZ403.R45B76 1992
615.8'52--dc20

Copyright © 1992
LifeRhythm
PO Box 806
Mendocino, CA, USA 95460
Tel: (707) 937-1825
Fax: (707) 937-3052

*Dedicated to
Hawayo K. Takata,
my master, teacher and friend.*

Table of Contents

From Phyllis Lei Furumoto, O Sensei

In Japan, each person "knows" Reiki. Reiki is the energy of living. This energy is honored and used in guiding daily life. Each part of life has a ceremony and tradition based on the understanding that Reiki is living energy. This attitude toward life has created disciplines—ways of living—within the Japanese culture. One of these "ways" or "arts" is the Usui System of Natural Healing. This System is a Healing Art, a way to wholeness by adopting a particular way of living.

Though the word Reiki now is used to identify the Usui System of Natural Healing, it is more accurate to say that we study the Usui System of Natural Healing in order to be with Reiki in our lives. The gift Reiki offers the "Western World" is a simple path to experiencing our lives as a sacred honorable experience.

An essence of oral tradition is the constant connection the student has to his/her teacher and mentor, the source of the tradition. This connection is not for validation, security or control. This connection is for guidance, to be used as a touchstone, as the student finds his/her own way through the maze of mind and belief.

Another essence is the natural changes and adjustments that are made in the stories and emphasis of the teacher depending on the student. This keeps the stories alive and dynamic. It is the lesson and the words remembered by the student that is the essence of the story, not the data.

Take this offering, use it wisely. Let the stories go to the place of wisdom within you. Allow your wisdom to guide your daily life.

Phyllis Lei Furumoto is the granddaughter of Hawayo Takata and lineage carrier of the Usui System of Natural Healing.

Preface

Takata's students have long wanted a book containing the stories she used to tell. I have been eagerly awaiting the opportunity to see the accomplishment of this legacy. In preparing to write about her stories, much research into the background of the culture and the various Buddhist practices at that time was done by Suzanne Rose, one of her students and now a practicing Reiki Master. Many conversations were held with some of Takata's students and masters in an effort to truly understand what her stories were saying. She told us "Listen and learn" and "Do it this way". But she never explained why or how. This is the manner of oral teachings from a master.

Ann Marie Mayhew and Ruth Scolnick helped me to clearly convey my ideas and thoughts. Dixie Shipp's contribution was the final organization of the stories. It was due to the efforts of all of us that these stories could be brought forth. We enjoyed this time in which each one, in turn, was brought closer to Takata, finding a deeper understanding of this priceless gift we know as Reiki.

Hawayo Kawamuru's parents came from Japan to live on Kawai and work in the sugar cane industry. This was the casual country style of living. The children went to the local schools and were expected to have a reliable job when they are teenagers. In 1915 they were not required to attend school beyond the age of fourteen. Hawayo Kawamuru had a good job and a good relationship with her employer in the household of the owner of the sugar cane plantation near Kapaa, so she continued to work instead of going on to high school.

In 1938 she had been healed by Reiki and wanted to be able to teach others how to use it for self-healing and to help others. She had met many travelers and worked with the staff in this large home, but she had no training to teach anything. She understood the background of the Reiki teachings in the same way that any ordinary person practicing Buddhism would know.

But how to convey this simple teaching to the people in Hawaii, some of whom were suspicious of anything not written in the Christian Bible? This was her challenge. A common way of teaching children was by telling a story to illustrate the point. Parables have been used the world over for that purpose.

Hawayo Takata used the story of Mikao Usui, told in parables, to convey her love and respect for this wonderful healing touch that had restored her health. Today we expect to be taught with accuracy, with names and dates documented. We are disappointed, even disillusioned, that her stories about Usui cannot be verified. The stories about Hyashi and herself have been verified. But I am grateful to those who have given me the facts in the life of Mikao Usui. Now I have a greater understanding of Takata and the healing method she taught me to use and to teach. The joy comes in finding the truth, which is the point for which she told the stories.

Hawayo K. Takata was a great lady, known, loved and respected by great numbers of people from all walks of life. She brought Reiki from Japan in 1936 and for thirty-five years she was the only master taching. She took the responsibility of seeing that Reiki was taught in the tradition in which she had been taught. Since 1975 her teachings have spread world-wide with the proliferation of masters. She most certainly is one of the people in this century who made great changes in the way people live and perceive themselves, making this world a better place to be.

I invite you to read these stories with the same sense of joy I experienced as I wrote them. Look for the essence of the teachings.

Fran Brown
San Mateo, California
October 1997

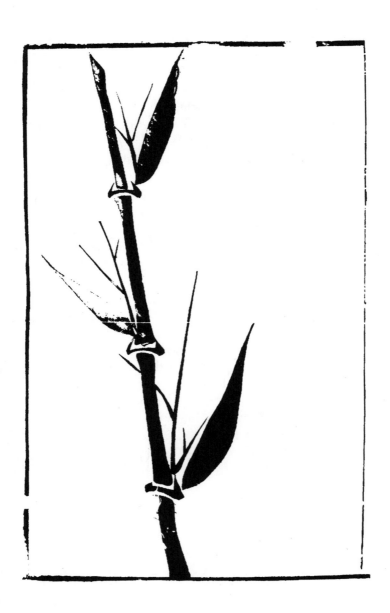

1

Early Years

"Let me tell you a story..."

It all began as dawn was just breaking over the Garden Isle of Kauai. The day would be Christmas Eve, 1900. In the home of a young Japanese couple, a mid-wife was helping the young mother deliver her third child. Many young people had come from Japan to this island of flowers to work in the flourishing cane industry, and this family was living in the village of Hanama-ulu, near Lihue.

The wail of a newborn babe announced its arrival. The midwife told the mother, "You have a strong, healthy baby girl."

When the mother looked at that tiny, squirming, wailing bit of humanity, she thought to herself, "If she is ever to amount to very much, she must have a very big name." Then the idea came to her to name her after the Big Island, Hawaii, changing the last letter to 'O' because girls names end in O.

With a sigh of relief, the young mother said, "Give her a bath and wrap her in a new blanket. Then face her to the sun, put your hand on her head and say three times, 'I NAME YOU HAWAYO'. And then say, 'success, success, success.'"

Thus was the beginning of the eighty year career of the one we know as Hawayo Takata, the woman who brought Reiki from Japan and introduced it to the rest of the world.

Pula Pula

Though much smaller than the other children her age, little Hawayo wanted to do everything the others did, and it was usually she who called the shots when they were playing games.

After they reached the age of thirteen, the school children would spend the summer vacation working in the cane fields, cutting the seedling tops off the cane which had been cut. When the supervisor shook her sack, he found Hawayo's sack to be only two thirds filled. She was simply too small to fill the sack to the top!

She sat down and cried in frustration that she would not be able to earn the good wages of thirteen cents a sack.

Two family friends saw her crying and came over to her and said, "Your courage deserves reward. We will take part of our lunch hour and see that your sacks are filled to the top."

At the end of August, a little locomotive pulling a cane car came to pick up the workers for the last time. All the students climbed onto the car to be taken home.

That is, all but little Hawayo. She called to them to wait a minute.

She cleared the leaves and trash from a small area and sat down, folding her knees. She raised her hands and looked at the sky and said,

"God, this is a prayer of thanks! All these months and days have been very hard, but you gave me protection and with the kindness of these people I have been able to experience the cutting of this pula-pula. Thank you for everything, but PLEASE, NEVER, NEVER LET ME COME BACK TO THE CANE FIELD AGAIN. PLEASE LET ME DO BETTER THINGS WITH MY HANDS." She bowed three times and kissed the ground.

Needless to say, such a ceremony was just the entertainment the students on the cane car needed to end the summer! They whooped and hollered and teased her all the way home.

SHOW GRATITUDE

The Soda Fountain

The man who drove the locomotive which pulled the cane car had observed what had taken place that last day in the cane field. He was also on the school board.

One Sunday he paid a visit to Hawayo's father.

"Kawamuru-San, the school principal has asked if Hawayo can come and stay with my family. We need two substitute teachers and can only get one. We would like for Hawayo to substitute teach first grade. She can do her grade work in the evening."

Her father gave his blessing. She got along well with the children and so she received a five dollar gold piece and a silver dollar on Fridays. This was a great help to her family.

The next summer, 1914, she went to the opening of the new general store in Lihue. That walk seemed every inch of twenty miles, though it was only seven.

In town, she saw a man she knew who had a soda fountain. As they talked, he asked her if she would like to earn some money by washing the soda glasses and ice-cream dishes. She thought this was a great idea. When the store was crowded with people, he asked her to help serve them.

By the end of the busy day, they both were very tired. And she had that seven mile walk ahead of her. He sensed what she was thinking and said to her, "Let me give you a ride home in my buggy. You have worked very hard today and you must be very tired." She protested that it would be out of his way, but was very glad that he had insisted.

After greeting her parents, he said to her father, "Hawayo was a great help to me today. She learns fast and is very capable. I need somebody full time and I would like to have her work for me. Would that be all right with you?"

She had finished the American school, but she continued in the Japanese school from six to eight in the morning. Then she walked the seven miles to her job at the soda fountain. In her spare time, she did filing in the office of the general store.

DO YOUR WORK HONESTLY

The Elegant Lady

There was a very elegant lady who would come in the store and leave a list of purchases to be picked up later by her chauffeur. Sometimes she would give the list to Hawayo, who would say, "Thank you ma'am. Have a nice day." and bow very low.

The elegant lady would smile as she left the store.

The first day she did that, the head of the department, an Hawaiian man, patted her on the head and told her, "This lady is from a very important family. She was born here and she married a European nobleman. Her father is the owner of a whole plantation. Not a partner like the others here. He owns the whole company. His children were all brought up in Europe. They are ladies and gentlemen."

One day the elegant lady asked Hawayo, "Do you have a vacation? You told me that you are staying in the church boarding school because your father works in Kealia. During your vacation, I can give you a job in my home in Kealia. I would love to have you. Your father and mother would be happy, too, I am sure. You could visit them for a whole day every Sunday. I will double the wages you earn here, and give you room and board and your clothing."

Now that was a VERY attractive offer!

Hawayo went to her boss and said,

"I know I have a very good job here. I plan to visit the elegant lady on my one week vacation and if she asks me to stay and makes me a very, very attractive offer, perhaps I cannot refuse her. In that case, can I be relieved of this job here?"

The boss thought for a minute and then said,

"Wel-l-l-l... I'm sure you will be very happy and she will be happy to have you. We don't want to see you go, but this is a business, and we have to please our customers, and she is one of our biggest customers. So I might release you."

Since her vacation was to start the next day, she asked, "Would you please write me a few words of recommendation?"

PROVIDE FOR YOUR SECURITY

The Wedding

The elegant lady lived in the most magnificent house that Hawayo had ever seen. It was a fine colonial mansion on fourteen acres with five cottages and out-buildings surrounded by a beautiful lawn and flowers, staffed by twenty-one servants. She never dreamed that one day she would supervise all these people or that her good relationship with the elegant lady would continue for twenty-four years.

Hawayo went to work for the elegant lady and loved every moment of it. Hawayo was less than five feet tall and very slender, with bright sparkling eyes. She was dressed in a beautiful kimono with an elaborate obi which made her look like a living Japanese doll. She was very polite and respectful as she met the many very interesting people who came from great distances to visit the elegant lady.

This lady also had in her employ a young Japanese accountant whom she felt needed a wife. And she hoped he and Hawayo would like each other. They did. On March 10, 1917, Saichi Takata and Hawayo Kawamuru were married, and they were very happy together. They had two little girls, the first one being born on the elegant lady's birthday, much to her delight.

Then Saichi became ill and went to Tokyo to the Maeda Clinic for treatment. In 1930, at the age of 34, he died of lung cancer. This was a great shock and terrible loss to the family and community, for Saichi was the first one of Asian descent to be appointed by the government as Welfare Director. He also began the practice of having the plantation owners pay the wages of the priest or minister who served their workers. His reasoning was that the plantation needed the workers and the workers needed the church. This created mutual respect. He also helped with the Boy Scouts, service clubs, and sports groups.

Near the end of his life, he told Hawayo, "With the law of evolution, everything goes through a change. Do not grieve. When you think I am gone, look up and smile. Then I will understand that you also understand what religion tries to teach. I want you to be free to travel, to embrace the earth, and make your own life. I don't want you to bury me on Kauai and worry about a grave in a hill."

She said to him, "I want you by my side to teach me, give me guidance, and courage. Then I shall not fail."

She always felt his presence when she needed him.

DO NOT WORRY

The Camphor Tree

She worked very hard to become financially able to care for her family. She had little rest, pushing herself to hide her grief, to the point where she had a nervous breakdown. She also had a painful abdominal condition, a uterine tumor which required surgery, and emphysema from asthma which prevented the use of an anesthetic. She felt desperate.

She would sit under the big camphor tree, look up into the sky and meditate and pray.

One day she prayed, saying, "God, if You have ears and eyes, please look at me in this sad position. I am not yet thirty-five years old, yet I feel like I'm sixty. I cannot walk upright because of the pain in my stomach. Often I cannot even breathe. I do not know how to overcome this, so show me the way if I am to survive. I need HELP. I am thankful to be alive, but God, make me strong; make me well; for I am ready to serve You."

In her head, she heard a voice out of the sky say, "Yes, you have many troubles. Listen well... the first thing is to take care of your health and that of your family. If you have good health, you shall have wealth, because you can work and you can earn. You shall have happiness, security and long life."

She bowed her head to the ground and said "Thank you, thank you. But I do not know how. Show me the way. I accept, I accept."

She didn't know how she said these words so loud, but they must have really reached the Universe, because three weeks later her life began a complete change.

One of her sisters died of tetanus. She was only twenty-five years old and married one year. This was too great a sorrow to write in a letter to her parents. She must go to Japan and deliver the message in person. Then she would go to Tokyo to the clinic where her husband had been treated.

PROMOTE GOOD HEALTH

Parents

Hawayo's parents, the Kawamurus, had immigrated to Kauai and for forty years had never returned to Japan for a visit. They decided 1935 was the time for them to return to Japan for a year's vacation.

Before they left Kauai, Hawayo said to them, "Repair your home, modernize. You have lived in Hawaii where you have conveniences. You know that everything in Japan is still very, very ancient. I want you to put a faucet in your kitchen so you can draw water from the tank, and not have to carry the water from the well. Have electricity so you can have light. And put in a water toilet. If you have those things you will be comfortable. So plan to stay a year."

Now she had to be the person to deliver this very, very sad message. It was her duty. She could not write to them and shock them. She must tell them gently, in person.

Her sister-in-law said she would come with her and show her the way to her parent's home in Yamaguchi. She would bring her two daughters as company for Hawayo's youngest daughter and be moral support for Hawayo with the sadness of the burden she was carrying.

Hawayo also carried her husband's ashes, hoping to give him a second funeral at Ohtani Temple.

On the boat, she met a Buddhist minister from Kona who was going to be a resident minister in Kyoto in the main temple. He was kind and very gentle and offered to take care of the urn for her until she should come to the temple, and attend a second funeral for Saichi Takata. Meanwhile, she had the duty to her parents to perform.

She felt that to have this relief and the kindness of strangers was a part of God's plan for her.

And so, Hawayo and her companions took the train for Yamaguchi.

When they arrived at her parent's home, her father and mother were so, so happy. Hawayo looked at her sister-in-law and with their eyes they said not today, not today. They are too happy. Love first, tomorrow duty.

The house was very cheerful. New shoji doors, new floor covering tatami, water faucet in the kitchen, and a closet on the porch enclosed a water toilet. How convenient for people from Hawaii! They talked of many things and her parents were so happy.

The next morning, the two women looked at each other and whispered, "after breakfast, yes, after breakfast."

They were preparing a beautiful breakfast with ingredients they had brought from Hawaii, Kona coffee and pancakes and Vienna sausage, when a man arrived on a bicycle.

He had a letter in his hand and he greeted her parents very kindly and very solemnly. He bowed very low, and after salutations he said, "I heard your daughter, Hawayo, returned from Hawaii, and I suppose by now you have heard the sad news about your other daughter's death. Oh, I'm sorry if you didn't know she had died. Did you get the message from Hawayo?"

Mr. Kawamuru's mouth dropped open.

The young women in the kitchen could hear the conversation. Her sister-in-law pushed Hawayo and said, "Now is the moment. Get out of the kitchen. Hang your head down low, and sit in front of your father. Bow your head. Let the head touch the floor, and say, I am sorry. Forgive me. You were too happy yesterday, and we did not want to spoil your day, but it is true about my sister. It is true. Just say this. And this way you don't have to say that she died or passed away. The man said it. So all you have to say is that it is true."

When she said, "It is true. It is true," she choked. It was very hard for the words to come out to say "forgive me" and "I am sorry." He waited a few seconds, and it was her father who put his hand on her shoulder and said, "Oh, you have suffered ten days and ten nights on the boat where you could see nothing but water and waves, and I am sure all the time you were thinking how you were going to break the news. How can I shed a tear? No more. I am not going to shed a tear. You did all the suffering, and I share with you. Dry your tears. Lift your head up."

Her mother spoke and said, "I, too, will not shed a tear. And so what are we doing here? We know now what happened to our daughter. Let us all wear shoes and hurry, hurry. Come on, let's go to church. We will offer her prayers and give her a mass. That is the only way she can be reached and she will appreciate it. So let's go to church. Get on your shoes, everybody." They left to get dressed for church.

The man was dumbfounded. He didn't know what to say. But he opened his mouth and said, "It's a very good idea. I will go on my bicycle and alert all the neighbors to be at church when you arrive. I'm sure the services will help everybody." And he left on his bicycle.

When the family arrived at the church the people were already there. They all were wearing their work clothes. They didn't stop to dress up for church, but they were there. The minister was at the door and he said, "Kawamuru-San, we heard, and we were expecting you. Please come in and sit down. The service will start immediately."

The services were beautiful, and they felt better. Afterward, the minister's wife served tea and cookies and they had a bit of conversation before they returned home.

After dinner that evening, Hawayo and her sister-in-law made plans to take her parents and the children down south to Beppu to the spas for five or six days. Then they would return to Hiroshima where Hawayo's grand-mother had a large house nearby with fruit orchards, rice paddies, vegetable gardens and even a small beach with clams and oysters.

They would spend several days there and leave her parents to enjoy a longer visit. Hawayo would go to Tokyo to the Maeda Clinic.

HONOR YOUR PARENTS

2

Takata Finds Reiki

Operation Not Necessary

Mrs. Takata entered the Maeda hospital in Akasaka. This was the hospital that had treated her husband and they welcomed her back again. Dr. Maeda took one look at her and promptly told her that she needed rest and comfort. His sister, the dietitian, would order good food for her and she should think of this place as a resort hotel. Rest, relax, have peace of mind, enjoy, and gain a few pounds. In three weeks, she was given a thorough examination along with x-rays and told, "You have a tumor, gall-stones and appendicitis. That's why your stomach aches all the time."

Surgery was scheduled for 7 o'clock the next morning.

The next morning, the nurse came and prepared her for the operation. Then she took her to the operating room and put her on the operating table. The surgical nurse was preparing the instruments needed for the operation. The doctors were washing at the sink. She could hear the water running and conversation, though she couldn't hear what they were saying. She was lying very still on the surgical table.

Then, all of a sudden, she heard a voice. She opened her eyes and looked around. The voice didn't seem to belong to anyone in the room, but it said, "Operation not necessary. Operation not necessary."

When she heard it the first time, she thought, "I am just nuts, I am crazy. I am hearing things."

But the second time she heard the voice, "Operation not necessary," she pinched herself, thinking, "If I feel the pinch, I must not be out of my mind. But if I hear it again, I'll believe it."

The voice was louder the third time. "OPERATION NOT NECESSARY." What to do now?

The voice said, "ASK, ASK, ASK."

"Ask whom?"

The voice came back with, "THE HEAD SURGEON, THE HEAD SURGEON, THE HEAD SURGEON," and the voice went away.

She got off the operating table and stood on the floor. The nurse saw her and came running after her saying,

"Look what you've done! We have to sterilize you all over again now. That's a big mess you have made of yourself. If you wanted to go to the toilet, you could have asked and I could have fixed you right on this bed!" and she pounded on the bed..."You've ruined everything!

"No, no bed pan." said Takata. "I want to see the doctor."

The doctor came in with towels over his hands after scrubbing for the surgery, and asked what the commotion was all about. When he saw her standing on the floor in the operating room, he said, "Look what you have done! Now, we have to start all over again."

Takata asked, "Is there another way?"

The surgeon asked, "Are you afraid you're going to die?"

She replied, "No. This is one of the best hospitals in Japan."

"Are you afraid of the surgery?"

"No. But tell me, is there another way?"

He said, "Yes. It all depends on how much time you have here in To-kyo. It may take weeks, months, even a year. Who knows? It all depends on how well you respond. My sister the dietitian will tell you about it."

The Reiki Clinic

The doctor's sister, the dietitian, had been in the Keo University hospital with a very severe case of dysentery. When she had gone into coma, they called her daughter at school and told her to come right away to see her mother.

As her daughter was leaving school, a girl friend stopped her and told her to go first to Dr. Hayashi's Reiki clinic, Shina No Machi, which was located across the street from the hospital.

Mrs. Hayashi greeted her, and the little girl explained that her grandfather, Dr. Maeda, was a professor of internal medicine and her mother was in the hospital in a coma and asked that he please come to the hospital with her and see if he could help her mother. Dr. Hayashi recognized the name as his own uncle and agreed to come immediately.

He gave her a Reiki treatment and she came out of the coma.

He gave her a Reiki treatment every day until she was able to go home. When she was stronger, she took the Reiki training.

This lady knew very well that Reiki was effective and so she took Takata to Hayashi's clinic.

After the greeting, Mrs. Hayashi showed them to a room with eight couches. At each couch, two practitioners were working on a client. When it was her turn, Takata lay on a couch. The gentleman who worked on her head told her that her eyes were taking a lot of energy. They needed to be revitalized. The other gentlemen was treating her stomach from the right side of her body and said, "I feel you have lots of pain in the area of the gall bladder."

A little lower he said, "You have a lump... could be a tumor, and I'm feeling a lot of bad vibrations around your appendix."

HOW COULD THEY TELL THAT? There was no time for the hospital to send around a diagnosis. She pinched herself to make sure she wasn't dreaming and decided to wait until tomorrow to ask questions.

Why were their hands so hot? And why did they vibrate slightly?

WHY WERE THEIR HANDS SO DIFFERENT?

When she went to the clinic the next day, she looked up to the ceiling to see if there was any connection from above. She saw none. So she dropped her purse on the floor to have an excuse to look under the couch to see if there were any wires. She saw none.

While the practitioner on her right was working on her stomach, she reached up and clapped his sleeve between her two hands. He was startled, but reached in the pocket of his sleeve and handed her a tissue saying, "If you wanted a tissue why didn't you ask?"

She said, "No, no tissue! Where is the battery?"

"What battery?"

"The battery, the machine!"

"I don't know what you are talking about!"

She said, "There are no wires coming down from the ceiling and no wires under the couch. But your hands are so hot. Where is the battery, the machine?"

Upon hearing this, everyone burst into laughter.

One practitioner laughed so hard that he fell off his low stool.

Dr. and Mrs. Hayashi came in to see what was so funny. Then they joined in the laughter.

The dignity and decorum of the clinic was gone!

DO NOT WORRY

The Way

Three weeks of daily Reiki treatments and she was much better. All aches and pains had disappeared, no more eye trouble. Her color was better than it had ever been and her strength was returning. Reiki was restoring her health.

In four months, the asthma and gall stones were gone. Takata's health was restored!

She felt that she must have Reiki to keep herself healthy.

When she asked her friend the dietitian if she could learn Reiki, she was told, "Reiki is a closely guarded Japanese treasure. It is for Japanese people only and you are an American. I think it is quite out of the question."

And American she certainly was! When she wanted to see something, she stopped and looked. When she wanted to know about something she asked.

This was not the manner of a Japanese lady. They were not to express feelings in public nor ask questions. If one was determined to know an answer, she might consider asking her husband later in the quiet of their home.

Respecting their customs, she said no more. But she was determined to find a way to learn Reiki.

She meditated and prayed for a way to learn Reiki.

One day, the head surgeon at the hospital asked her how she was doing.

She told him, "I had a reaction after the fourth treatment. For fourteen days and nights, I went to the bathroom, bathroom, bathroom. So much I had to crawl back to my room. And the smell was awful! So bad! And I could only eat soft rice and drink green tea. I was able to walk for the first time on December 24, my birthday. And on December 25th, I was a different person. The asthma and all the aches and pains were gone. I have no more head trouble, no more eye trouble, just feel great, and light as a feather. My whole body is rejuvenated. I have gained fourteen pounds and lost ten years. I can walk as much as I like and run and I can blow like the wind. I have the best color ever and I am getting stronger every day. I am taking these treatments, I am getting well, and I want to learn Reiki. Please, doctor, help me."

"Ah, that's another story," he said. "They have rules. I think the association does not want to accept outsiders. There's nothing I can do."

"Yes, you can!" she quickly replied. "Because you are the greatest humanitarian, I know you can help. So, please, tell Dr. Hayashi that Takata came here to get well and she is seeking health, but she cannot come to Japan every time she needs a treatment. So while she's here, she wants to learn Reiki, and she will help herself and her family. All she wants to do is help herself and the family, so that she can stand on her own feet and support her family so that the family can live a little longer. They are losing children when they are twenty years old, eighteen years old, and twenty-five years old and that is too, too sad a life. Too sad. And I am only thirty-five and I don't want to die. You have to stress that point and say 'Dr. Hayashi, save a life, save a family.' You can say it because you are a great, great man."

He folded his arms and looked sharply into her eyes, knitted his brows and said, "Ah so, I see you mean it. You are sincere. Are you willing to pay the price?"

Her reply to him was, "If I can buy my life, why not? Without life, I am nobody. I am nothing. If I can, I shall."

He asked her how she planned to pay for it. She replied, "I've got a house. I'm gonna sell it and I'll send you the money."

He was concerned, "But then you won't have a roof over your head."

Her reply was instantaneous, "Don't worry about that. When I come to that point, I'm gonna do the worrying. Don't you worry about that. No. That's nothing. I'm only thirty-five years old. When I am fifty and when I am well, nothing. I'm only thirty-five years old. When I am fifty and when I am well, I might have two houses. But what is one house if I die? I have nothing. So please, doctor."

He had a serious look on his face as he said, "Yes, I'm going to try. I can't promise, but I'm going to try. Tomorrow morning, stop at the office. You will find a letter. Take it to Dr. Hayashi. Give it to Mrs. Hayashi."

Instead of giving the letter to his secretary to type, the good doctor wrote the letter personally.

By hand. With a brush. On a scroll about two and a half yards long.

When Dr. Hayashi opened the letter, he was very impressed.

He said, "Ah. I cannot ignore this letter. I am highly honored by such a hand-written letter from such a great surgeon. And he is asking me on a humanitarian basis to save Takata and the family because I know her condition. She lives so far away. She needs it in the worst way. Then she can help herself and her family. That will be a very great and noble thing that Reiki can do."

He called a meeting of the *Usui Light Energy Research Association* and showed them the letter. He explained how he felt and asked if they agreed with him that it would be a good thing to let Takata become a Reiki practitioner.

And so, Takata was given permission to learn Reiki... after exacting from her the promise to stay in Japan and work in the Reiki Clinic every day for one year.

BE KIND TO ALL

Takata's Reiki Year

Now that her health was restored and she was given permission to be in the next Reiki Practitioner's class, she took care of the family details of her life. Then she moved into Dr. and Mrs. Hayashi's home where she would stay during her year of internship.

Along with the other Reiki students, she was initiated to receive the Universal Life Energy by Dr. Hayashi. He explained that this would be done in four small steps, taking four days to complete the First Degree of Reiki.

On the first day, the class was taught the basic positions for treatment above the neck—the head, eyes, ears, nose and throat—and the conditions and diseases which might be found in these areas.

They were taught to stop bleeding noses, to treat eye ailments and diseases of the mouth, such as cancer and canker sores. They also learned to vitalize thyroid glands and to stop any inflammation of the throat and tonsils, as well as diphtheria.

The second day teachings were how to treat the front of the body, the chest, heart, liver and gall bladder, the pancreas, stomach, small intestines, colon, and bladder, as well as the uterus and ovarian glands for women.

In later years, when she was teaching, she would say, "Spend half your treatment time here because this is the main factory. It processes the fuel taken in and delivers it to the places it is needed."

The third day, the lesson was for the back, the spine, sympathetic nerves, lungs, adrenal glands, kidneys, spleen, and for the men, the prostate gland. They were shown where and how to place their hands to permit the Life Energy to flow into the body of the client in order to balance the condition or ailment.

On the fourth day, Dr. Hayashi would discuss how to heal acute cases and accidents. He also would spend much time talking about the spiritual side of Reiki, discussing in detail the Five Ideals put forth by Dr. Usui.

1. DO NOT ANGER.
2. DO NOT WORRY.
3. COUNT YOUR BLESSINGS; honor your parents, your teachers and your neighbors; show appreciation for your food and do not waste.
4. EARN YOUR LIVING HONESTLY.
5. BE KIND TO EVERYTHING THAT HAS LIFE.

They were taught there is always a cause and an effect. Remove the cause and there shall be no effect. Reiki will work as long as the practitioner believes it, applies it, and continues to use it.

They each were given a list of complaints and places to look for their cause.

In her later years of teaching, past experience had demonstrated to her that it was better to decline to give out any printed matter or to allow taping or notes taken during her classes. She felt notes would encourage practitioners to diagnose and prescribe and that is to be left to the medical profession.

Internship

Events at Hayashi's Shina No Machi went according to a schedule that had worked well for years. The year of Takata's internship was no exception. Each morning from seven o'clock until twelve, the practitioners gave treatment to all who came to the Clinic. They worked in pairs, sixteen practitioners treating eight clients. Whenever the treatment for a client was finished, there was another waiting to be treated. They took an hour for lunch and then went out on house calls individually. Each practitioner would go to a home and give a treatment of one hour to one hour and a half.

Sometimes, they would ride a train for several hours to reach the home of the person to be treated. Their clients came from all walks of life. Takata accompanied Dr. Hayashi to give Reiki treatments in some very luxurious homes. She even had the opportunity to treat a little princess.

They were usually home by seven o'clock in the evening. Takata would find hot water ready for a bath and a hot dinner prepared.

At the end of the year of her internship when she came for her examination, Dr. Hayashi gave her his opinion of the way she had performed as a practitioner in the Reiki Clinic. He told her that whenever she was sent out on a house call, she never got lost though she did not know Tokyo. The client always called after she finished giving the treatment and told Dr. Hayashi what time she had arrived, how the treatment had gone and what time she had left. She had treated successfully many different kinds of problems. She had passed her internship with flying colors and was ready to be a practitioner.

Dr. Hayashi congratulated her and told her that she was now ready for the Oku Den, or second degree... if she could afford it.

In 1936, she paid five hundred US dollars for Second Degree training and then returned to Kauai.

HONOR YOUR TEACHER

Occasionally, Takata referred to herself as a "country-jack." She was always very honest in her dealings with people. When she wanted to know something; she asked directly, but with tact. She respected the feelings of others and was very accommodating with people. Having her as a house guest was very comfortable. She was adaptable to the hospitality offered her and she always gave a special blessing to the home where she spent a night. She was also very trusting... she considered that everyone else was just as honest and trustworthy as she valued herself to be... and this trait made her vulnerable to those who would sometimes take advantage of her...

Sadie

One day, Takata met a lady from Hawaii who was depressed and so lacking in energy that she could not take good care of her business. Feeling sorry for her, Takata gave her treatment in her apartment for a week. Then she took her to Dr. Hayashi's Clinic and told her to come there until she recovered her health.

Takata soon found that she had many mental worries too. As she treated her, Takata talked of returning to Hawaii and the projected visit there by Dr. Hayashi and his daughter.

With a deep sigh, Sadie, the lady, said, "I wish I could go home. If I go back to Hawaii, all my troubles will be over."

Takata asked, "Why aren't you free to go home?"

Sadie replied, "I have opened my shop and I would like to stay here until I know I can leave it in good hands. So I have many worries." Takata commented, "The winter must be very hard for you. You would recover much more quickly in Hawaii."

Sadie said, "But I do not have the means to return to Hawaii."

Takata told her, "Well, I will help you."

When the day came that she was well again, she said to Takata, "I'm very grateful to you. Don't worry, I will go back to Honolulu and I will be able to pay you."

When Takata arrived in Yokohama to take the boat to Hawaii, she saw Sadie sitting on a suitcase, crying. She asked her, "Why the tears? Aren't you happy to be going home?"

Between sobs, Sadie wailed, "My creditors say that I cannot leave here."

"Creditors?"

"Yes, in order to open the shop, I borrowed money and they want to know who will be responsible."

Takata asked, "Well, when you go back to Hawaii, don't you think you can send the money?"

Sadie answered, "I am sure I can. But not the first month, because I don't know what my position will be in Honolulu."

Takata asked, "Just for now, how much?"

"Two hundred and fifty dollars."

"Well, I can help you, then. But be sure to pay your creditors every month when you reach Honolulu."

She promised. And so, Takata helped her out and she was able to take the same boat. In fact, the two women were assigned to the same stateroom.

Towards morning, just before arrival, Takata became violently ill. She called to Sadie, but she was not there. She went to the bathroom, back and forth, back and forth, and finally had to crawl back to her bed.

One of the stewards found her in the hallway and asked her if she was sick. He helped her back to bed.

The next morning, when they arrived in Honolulu, the purser helped her to the dining salon, sat her in a chair, and told her that if the immigration inspector asked her what was the matter to say that she was seasick. Otherwise the ship might be quarantined.

"Seasick" Takata was sent back to her stateroom, and there she stayed until she asked the hotel to send someone for her. On shore, she went to a doctor who said it was ptomaine poison or something very, very harsh in the stomach. She was so weak that she had to rest for a week before continuing to Kauai.

Kapaa

In 1936, when Takata had completed her year practicing Reiki in Hayashi's Shina No Machi Clinic in Tokyo, and had made the boat trip back home to Kauai, she had no intentions of doing Reiki professionally, however, this did come about after she was able to help her dear family and friends. She immediately began to offer her services to those in need of healing. Gradually, word spread of her ability and willingness to treat them and people began to seek her help.

Her first patient was her brother-in-law who suffered chronic stomach and digestive trouble

A little five year old girl who had undergone two operations for mastoiditis was in need of another operation to drain her mastoids. Takata gave her the regular treatment, spending more time on the swollen area. It soon came to a head, and the previous scar opened itself and drained for five days. On the sixth day, the fluid was clear and the wound closed up. Her overall health improved and the next year she attended kindergarten with no more signs of trouble.

A middle aged man had an appendix operation that did not heal and needed to be drained by a tube, requiring him to remain in the hospital. She went to the hospital and gave him Reiki treatments, especially in the area of the pancreas. There was good drainage, and in four days, he was discharged. His self-healing was slow because he was diabetic.

There was a person with seventeen years of chronic asthma. After four months of treatments he was fully recovered, had gained weight, and was able to work full time as a carpenter and painter.

Word got around quickly in this small town and on this small island. One morning, Takata opened her front door and found ten people waiting for her attention. Each one wanted to be the first one she would see. One came from sixty miles away. Another claimed to be suffering the most. And so it went.

Takata didn't know how to handle that situation, so she called the local postmaster, a family friend, to organize them. There were too many for one day, so he told them to go home and read the local newspaper. When Takata had an office ready, they should call for an appointment and she would be able to see them all in due time. He also advised Takata to get a license, rent a place to give treatments, install a telephone, and see them only by appointment.

In October, 1936, she opened her office in Kapaa.

More Sadie

A month later, Dr. Hayashi and his daughter arrived in Kauai... accompanied by Sadie, who "came to keep them company because they are strangers."

They had one class and Sadie said, "Hurry up on to Honolulu. There is no time to waste on this small island. The people in Honolulu are just waiting for you and I will help to advertise."

The Hayashis and Takata stayed in a hotel in Honolulu. Each day at breakfast, they were joined by Sadie and her husband... who charged their breakfasts to Takata. When she discovered this, she told the hotel she only wanted to pay for the Hayashis and herself.

Takata found a hotel where she could rent two cottages. The manager told her, "You and your daughter can have one cottage and Dr. Hayashi and his daughter the other cottage. There is enough room that you can interview people and teach Reiki classes there."

The next morning after breakfast, they took their baggage to the new hotel cottages. When they arrived, the manager was not there and the porter told them he had orders not to let them in.

They were not accepted! With that, he put their suitcases out on the sidewalk.

Takata was confused, humiliated, and a stranger in town. She walked down the street to another hotel and found the manager to be a man whom she knew from Kauai. He took them to another hotel where they settled into two cottages for the next four months.

Takata rented the YMCA or YWCA, and free lectures about Reiki were given by Dr. Hayashi with Takata demonstrating. There was newspaper coverage and the public gradually came to know about Reiki.

On Saturday, Sadie came to Takata and asked to borrow twenty-five dollars. She said, "Because you paid my fare and brought me back home to Honolulu, my husband is very angry and he won't let me have a penny. So you have to lend me twenty-five dollars." Each Saturday she came and borrowed twenty-five dollars.

One Saturday, the hotel owner saw Sadie asking Takata for money. He said to Sadie, "I don't want your kind of people in my hotel. Please leave and don't come back again."

When she thought things over, she realized how Sadie had taken advantage of her. She swallowed her tears and reminded herself that she was just another country girl in a city.

Then Sadie asked for money for a ticket to return to Japan. Takata gave it to her, thinking it worth the cost to have her leave the country. Four hours later, the lady returned and asked for money for the ticket again, saying she had spent the other money just given her for clothes. After all, she could not return to Japan with the same clothes she had brought out of Japan with her.

This was the last straw! Takata was furious!

She turned to Dr. Hayashi and said, "This this this this this thing that is happening... can I get mad just this one time? I know I am a country jack and she is biting me all over. I just want to use my elbow grease and give her a punch in the eye and knock her down the stairs so she can't come back any more!"

Hayashi said, "If you fly off the handle you will be hurting yourself. So do not anger." He smiled and turned the other way.

Takata took a deep breath and told herself "I will not anger today." Very gently, she said to Sadie, "Do you see that doorway, and the veranda beyond, and the six steps down to the walkway? Please go down there and out the gate and never come back to me again. I have no ears to hear you."

Takata was determined to live by the Reiki ideals.

DO NOT ANGER

The Exorcist

A widow and her daughter lived at the edge of a cane field. The daughter had been ill and was growing more disturbed in her thinking as time went on. The widow decided to look for help for her daughter. She talked to a Filipino kahuna about her daughter's illness and he told her that she was being possessed. He could remove the possessing spirit from her with a ceremony that would cost her one hundred dollars. She paid him and made an appointment for the ceremony.

On a Saturday, the kahuna arrived with two ladies to help. They began the ceremony with chanting. One of them beat on a pan and the other two shook rattles. Then they began to dance, raising their voices loud and clear. As they danced around inside the house with the widow and her daughter inside, they began to stomp heavily and to shout at the top of their voices to drive out the possessing spirit.

All this stomping made the house shake and coins and money began to fall from in between the wooden boards of the walls and ceiling. You see, the widow had no confidence in banks and hid her money in the cracks in the house.

Her neighbors, hearing all the loud voices, stomping, beating on pans, and the poor girl screaming as the coins rained down upon them all, gathered around the house to see what was going on. Cane workers carrying their machetes on their way home gathered in the crowd to see if the widow needed help.

One of the supervisors was looking out over the fields when he saw the gathering around the widow's house. As he looked closer, he saw the machetes. He could even hear the noise in the distance and he began to worry that there was trouble brewing. It could be an uprising or a strike forming. Whatever it was, it looked like BIG TROUBLE.

He decided it was best to notify the military.

The shouting, stomping, chanting, and screaming were still going on, making quite a ruckus, when three jeeps filled with armed marines appeared on the scene.

They invited the kahuna and his helpers to consider their work concluded and leave the widow and her daughter to clean up the mess. When the neighbors saw that the two ladies were all right, they went home.

When things had calmed down from this affair, Takata offered to help the girl through her illness. Reiki is quiet, calm, and relaxing. With treatments, the girl was restored to good health.

BE KIND TO ALL

Sadie's Revenge

When Takata finished her quiet admonition that Sadie leave and never return, Sadie was furious. As she went down the steps she turned around and shook her finger at Takata and said, "I'll fix you!" and she ran down the walk and out the gate.

The hotel manager told Takata that she would probably go to the police and make a report and then they would come and question Takata and Hayashi.

Sure enough, Sadie went to Immigration and told the officers there, "Dr. Hayashi and Miss Hayashi came to Hawaii as tourists and they are holding lectures and collecting money."

Takata became very concerned. She imagined that the Hayashis, poor dears, would be taken out and shot.

Dr. Hayashi continued his consultations with people in a private room. About ten people were sitting around when two Caucasian men came in. One was a driver and the other a well dressed businessman who sat down and opened a newspaper, holding it in front of his face as he spoke. He said, "I came to see Dr. Hayashi."

Takata replied, "Oh, but he is very busy now."

"He has consultations?"

"Yes. People are here."

"How much does he charge?"

"Nothing. Everything is free."

"Even the consultation?"

"And he gives it to you in private. First come, first served. You have to wait your turn. It seems you are the last one to come in, so you have to wait until the others are through."

"Very well, I've got the time."

She asked him, "May I ask what is your problem?"

Then he said, "I have stomach trouble, I have so much stomach trouble."

Takata told him, "Oh is that so... well, that's all right. he will be able to help you. I'm sure you'll be happy you came here."

In about ten minutes this man began to get really sick, he had a terrific stomach ache which would not permit him to stand up or lie down, cramps and all. And so, he told his driver, "Take me to the hospital, quick, quick. Pretty soon you will have to drag me out, I won't be able to walk!"

The driver brought the car to the door, put him in the car and they went to the hospital.

One of the women who had been waiting for consultation went outside and returned saying, "Mrs. Takata, you are surrounded by spies. There's a policeman outside this hotel and when I came out he said, "What did Hayashi do to you?"

"I told him, 'Oh, I asked him questions in consultation.' and he said, 'Did he give you a satisfactory answer?' 'Yes.' 'Are you very happy? How much did he charge?' 'Free, no charge.'"

This policeman was writing in shorthand. But this young woman was an excellent student of shorthand and she could read what he was writing. She grabbed the book he was writing in and tore it into pieces, saying, "You big crook. You are putting down all false statements. Goodness, what a shame." And she threw the paper scraps into the wind and watched them blow all over the place.

She said, "Mrs. Takata, you have spies around this hotel."

Soon two policemen came and the policeman taking notes went away with them.

In an hour, two policemen appeared, asking for Takata. Then the questioning began.

"Are you Takata?"

She answered, "Yes."

"Do you have guests?"

"Yes."

"Where are they?"

"Right here."

"They have to go to Immigration to be questioned."

She told Dr. Hayashi, "Be certain to get an interpreter so that there can be no mistake in your replies. Also, tell them that I will say no more except through my lawyer. And I will get a lawyer for you. So you say that you want to talk to a lawyer."

The policeman made a threatening gesture at Takata and told her, "You shut up!"

It was lunch time, but nobody could eat for thinking of the terrible ordeal the Hayashis were being put through. In an hour, they returned, Dr. Hayashi wearing his customary smile as he described what had happened.

He had approached the immigration officer with, "I don't know why I am called here. I am not a laborer. I am a first class tourist and I have a visa to that effect. I have a passport, first class. If you do not want visitors, I have a country to go back to. I have a home there and I live very comfortably. I don't have to be here."

The officer asked, "In that case, why are you giving lectures and collecting money?"

Hayashi replied, "That is a false report. As you have seen in the papers, the lectures are free. Everybody is welcomed. The public is invited. I can show you the ad."

The officer answered, "Well, the report stated that although this is the way it is advertised in the papers, the people were giving you envelopes and passing the hat for collections."

Hayashi answered him, "That is false. I have never done that. And why didn't you send somebody in plain clothes to come into the lectures and see if I did that.? Are you going to believe others or are you going to believe me?"

The officer then asked Hayashi, "How much money do you have?"

Hayashi said, "Well, if you were going to talk about money, why didn't you ask me at the hotel. I don't carry all my money with me just because I am coming here. But I do have some money with me. Here are my traveler's cheques. I have used three hundred dollars already. But this is for one thousand dollars. Bought in Japan, not Honolulu. See, it has the imperial stamp from the Bank of Tokyo. My daughter has her own. I have brought six of these. Do you want to see the rest? Come to my hotel and I will show them to you. The inspector's face got very red. In 1937, six thousand dollars was a great deal of money for a tourist to bring to Hawaii. He said that the report was entirely different. The report was filed by a woman named Sadie."

The investigation over, the official apologized saying, "We have to follow up on reports when they are filed."

Then the story came out in the papers. There was a big article. The man who came in for a consultation and became really ill with a stomach ache was playing a phony part. He could not stay in Honolulu because we knew who he was.

With all these issues cleared up, the editor of the paper said, "I am going to write very good articles. Go ahead and get the halls, your halls are going to be filled with lectures and classes, classes, classes."

Takata was the demonstrator and Hayashi was the lecturer. He always sat on a chair and lectured. That was November and December. In those two months, they really had a beautiful crowd.

The people felt very sorry for Hayashi and Takata. They came to the lecture and saw how small was this young lady who had so much to overcome. They said, "You tiny thing. Here you were from the country and the city mouse tried to bite the country mouse."

Great things happened because the people responded. Hawaii was a territory and immigration was federal, so the report of all this went up to Congress. Mr. Wilder King was a delegate to congress at that time, and he handled this case. He telephoned her in December to say, "Takata, you've won the case. Your friends are free to stay through February, the limit of their visas."

DO YOUR WORK HONESTLY

Hayashi's Announcement

Before they left Hawaii in February 1938, there was a very big banquet attended by the many friends the Hayashi's had made in Honolulu. It was a gala affair held at a tea house, on February 22.

He received many presents. There was a koa cane, koa bowls and about one hundred and fifty leis made of hoa seed, ribbons and feathers—things that he could take home with him, since fresh flower leis would perish.

He was asked to speak to them and he took the opportunity to describe all the good things he had found there and the good people he had met. He said, "I want to say thank you, folks. As a teacher, a master, I have a student, Hawayo Takata, a Kauaian now in Honolulu. As of now, Takata is a Reiki Master. She has had many tests and has lived up to the principles. I ask you to give her your support. She is the Master and she can carry on."

Then Takata took the microphone and said, "I appreciate everything my teacher has taught me. I am highly honored and from here on, I need your support. I will be very happy to serve as your humble servant."

The next day, Dr. Hayashi and the hotel manager went to the radio station and he made the announcement on the radio that "Takata is the Reiki Master for this area and Japan and if I should go, Takata has been chosen to carry on this work."

Before leaving Japan to come to Hawaii, Dr. Hayashi had initiated both his wife and Takata as Reiki Masters, but he had waited to make the announcement in Hawaii.

His parting words to Takata were, "When I send for you, *you come!*"

Hayashi Sensei - Visit to Hawaii 1938

Takata Sensei 1938

The Gift

About sixteen months after opening her office in Kapaa, Hawayo had dinner with her father and spent the night in her sister's home.

Some time after midnight and before dawn, a strange feeling took place. It seemed that she was floating and she had no control except to wake up and hold onto the bed. Soon, she was gliding through the door without opening it, into the dining room and then the living room and settling gently onto the couch. She awakened her sister by calling to her and asked her to "Come quickly and put your hands on my chest and stomach and hold me down. I'm afraid I'll float through the ceiling and soar away into space!" This new experience was very frightening!

Was this to be the end of her life? She began talking to her sister about her unfinished family obligations, the things that come to mind when a person feels life is coming to an end, finishing her business. Her brother-in-law woke up, came into the parlor, and hearing and seeing the strange happenings, called the doctor.

The loud click of the gate as the doctor came in brought her out of the spell. Her sister was still tearfully holding her down on the couch. Takata stopped floating and was now lying on her back on the couch.

She told the doctor what had been happening. He was serious when he earnestly said that he had heard of such things as astral projections and levitations, but never had witnessed one. He checked her over and found no fever, pulse was normal. He stayed a while to chat and told her to report to his office in the morning. When she arrived, he checked her over and could find nothing abnormal.

She was hearing conversations from the subtle world, and in a few months, she became clairvoyant. She could see things taking place miles away.

She saw someone in a hospital twenty miles away. She called the district nurse to find out if she was correct or just plain crazy. The nurse investigated and found she was correct in every detail.

Next, she saw a patient calling for help in a hospital over eighty miles away. It was seven o'clock in the evening, visiting hours at the hospital. The radio was playing loudly, and no one could hear his buzzer. He had undergone a hernia operation earlier that day and was partially off his bed, struggling to keep from falling, and pressing his buzzer for help.

She called a friend in that district and asked him to check with the hospital and call her back and tell her if she was correct. In twenty minutes, the phone rang and he told her she was correct and the patient was very grateful for her help.

Another time, she saw a woman sitting on the hospital steps crying her heart out. She also saw the woman's two year old child undergoing surgery to drain fluid from her abdomen. The district nurse arrived to console the mother and father during this unexpected surgery. When the child was back in her bed, the nurse left the hospital and went to see Takata. She reported details just as Takata had seen them and said, "I think it is wonderful that you can see all these things happen."

But Takata was beginning to think this was not such a wonderful talent to have. She was seeing people in need of help, including accidents. And she dreaded nightfall, because she didn't want to spend the night looking at all those pictures. She needed to sleep. She decided to sit up in her closet all night, and maybe she could close out all those needs so she could get some sleep. Finally, she went back to Japan to see her teacher.

Hayashi told her, "It is your inner talent, something you were born with. The stronger and purer your system becomes, the more you are able to focus farther and farther into space. You must choose whether to be a healer or a clairvoyant." She decided to give up the clairvoyance and simply be a channel for healing. She could practice Reiki and sleep well at night!

In several months, she had returned to her comfort zone.

DO NOT WORRY

3

Reiki Origins

This is the way Takata told the story of Dr. Usui and the discovery of Reiki.

Mikao Usui

Dr. Usui was the head of a Christian boy's school in Japan toward the end of the last century. He delivered the Sunday sermon since he was also a minister.

One Sunday, some of the boys on the front row interrupted him by asking, "Dr.Usui, do you believe what the Bible says?"

He replied, "I studied the Bible very thoroughly while in the seminary here in Japan, and I have faith in what it says."

The boy speaking said, "We are just beginning our lives and would like for you to answer a question. Do you believe Jesus healed?"

Dr. Usui answered, "Yes."

"Then, please give us a demonstration by healing a blind person or a cripple, or by walking on water."

Dr. Usui responded, "I am a good Christian and have faith, but I can't demonstrate any of those things because I wasn't taught how."

The boys said, "We do not want to live in blind faith. We want to see one demonstration."

Dr. Usui said, "Some day, I would like to prove it to you. Some day, when I find a way, I will come back and show you. Right now I resign and tomorrow I shall go to America to study the Bible in a Christian country and then I shall come back."

He said "Good-bye" and left the church.

He entered a university in Chicago and studied philosophy, Christianity and the Bible. He found that the teachings were the same as he had been taught in the school taught by missionaries that he had attended as a growing boy and in the Japanese seminary. He could not find where Jesus left the formula for producing healing in others.

He continued his studies in Hinduism, Buddhism, and the other religions of the world. He learned that Gautama Buddha healed the blind, those with tuberculosis and leprosy.

By this time, he had been in Chicago for seven years. He returned to Kyoto to study more about Buddha in the hope of finding the formula for healing. Nara was the seat of Buddhism but Kyoto had the most temples and monasteries. He went to all of them always asking the same question, "Do the sutras say that Buddha healed?"

Always the same reply, "It is written."

"Can you do it?"

"In Buddhism, we consider the purpose of the ministry is to teach how to attain peace of mind, to realize happiness. The work of the church is to provide services that lead their minds to be more spiritual, for the spirit is eternal. Then they will want to show gratitude. This keeps us very busy. Physical illness is from the mind. The physical body is only temporary, and there are doctors and medicines to treat it."

After months of searching, he was referred to a Zen temple near Kyoto which had the largest Buddhist library in Japan. He asked to speak to the highest monk. As they talked, he observed that this seventy-two year old monk's face was young and lovely like a child's, and he had a very kindly voice as he said, "Come in."

Dr. Usui asked him, "Do the Zen believe in healing? Can you heal the physical self?"

"Not yet," was the monk's answer. "We are very busy attuning the mind first. We meditate every day for spiritual enlightenment."

"How are you going to get the physical training?" asked Dr. Usui.

"It will come. We have faith and some day in our meditation we will receive the method. Before I go into transition, I'm sure I will know how."

Dr. Usui then asked if he could enter the monastery and learn Buddhism. During the three years he was there, he read all the sutras written in Japanese and he sat for many hours in meditation with the monks. But this was not enough. He thanked them and was about to leave when the highest monk asked him to continue to study with them.

Research shows that at this time, this monastery was engaged in translating the earliest Sanskrit sutras from India into Japanese.

The monk said, "We have adopted Chinese characters, but it is like you reading Latin."

Dr. Usui stayed on for many years, learned to read Chinese and read the sutras that were written in Chinese. Still, he didn't find the formula he was searching for.

He studied Sanskrit and began reading the sutras written in Sanskrit, one of the first written languages.

It was in the sutras written in Sanskrit that he found some symbols and some phrases that might be the formula for Buddha's Manual Healing System! Simple and as plain as math! Written 2500 years ago!

The next problem was to put these things together so that they would make a practical, usable form. For this, he decided to undertake a fast and meditation in the hope of receiving a vision that would explain everything to him.

His parting words, as he left the monastery, were to come looking for his body if he was not back in twenty-two days.

His Meditation

With only a goatskin of water, he climbed Mt. Kurayama. He found a suitable pine tree within earshot of a stream, and there, he sat down to meditate. He gathered twenty-one stones beside him and each day at dawning he threw away one stone. He read sutras, chanted, prayed and meditated.

The early hours of the twenty-first day, in the darkest of night before dawn, when there could be seen neither moon nor stars, he finished his meditation. He opened his eyes and looked at the dark sky, thinking that this was his last opportunity to find the answer he had searched for all of these years.

He saw flashes of light... a phenomenon.

Light moved very fast toward him.

Excited and elated, he thought, "This is a test. I will face it."

With his eyes wide open, he saw the light strike him in the forehead. He fell backwards and lost consciousness. It was as if he died. His vision began as dawn was beginning to break. He looked to the right. Millions of bubbles in the colors of the rainbow were dancing in front of him.

Then the color red came from the right moving to the left and filled the whole sky. It held for a moment and then faded away. Then orange filled the sky... held for a moment... then faded away. Then yellow, then green, blue and purple. The whole sky was like a rainbow!

This was a phenomenon not to be forgotten!

When the last color had faded, a white light came from the right and formed a screen in front of him. Some of the things he had studied in Sanskrit appeared in golden letters in front of him. Then a golden symbol approached from the right, moved onto the screen, then moved off the left side as another symbol came into sight, then another, followed by yet another, until all the symbols had danced in front of him, and with all this came the understanding of their meaning and the use to be made of them.

Then he heard "Remember. Remember. Remember."

When he came to, it was daylight. He sat up and thought about all he had seen and heard.

He closed his eyes and all the golden letters and symbols appeared to him.

His First Miracles

He stood up. He felt strong. He wasn't hungry. He was full of energy and ready to walk back to the monastery. He felt it was a miracle that he felt so good.

He picked up his hat and cane, threw away his last stone and started down the mountain.

As he walked down the path, he stumbled on a rock tearing his toenail back. Blood flowed... and it hurt. He grabbed the toe with his hand and held it. He felt a pulse of energy. Then the pain went away. He removed his hand and saw the dried blood, but no problem with the toe. The toenail was in its proper place.

This was the second miracle.

When he reached the foot of the mountain, he walked until he saw a bench with a red blanket, and there he sat down.

In Japan a hundred years ago, when you wanted to travel you had to walk. Very few had horses. Whenever a house was willing to serve food to the passers-by, a red blanket was placed on a bench and an ash tray at hand, or a red table cloth was placed on a table with a bench.

An old man wearing an apron was firing up an hibachi (charcoal stove). Dr. Usui asked him if he might have some leftover rice, some salted plums and hot tea. The old man told him he would have to wait for rice gruel to be ready. Dr. Usui repeated his request for cold rice. And the old man insisted that he had to wait for the warm gruel. When Dr. Usui asked again for the cold rice, he received this reply from the old man.

"What you need is warm rice gruel, tea, miso, and pickled cabbage. Judging from the direction from whence you have come, a favorite mountain for meditation, and the length of your beard, you have just finished a twenty-one day fast. And you do not want to break a fast of that length with yesterday's cold rice. Sit down, and I will send your breakfast to you when it is ready."

Dr. Usui reached for the rice box and took it to the bench with him and sat down to wait.

The old man's grand-daughter, a pretty teen-aged girl brought his breakfast to him. She was wearing a scarf under her chin tied on top of her head like rabbit ears, and there were tear stains on her swollen cheeks beneath her red yes.

Dr. Usui asked her what was the matter. She replied, "I have a terrible tooth-ache. It has been hurting for three days and I cannot go to the dentist because it is seventeen miles to the dentist's office and I have no way to get there."

Dr. Usui felt very sorry for the girl and asked if he could put his hands on her cheeks. He felt around her jaw and asked "Is this it? Is this the one that is bothering you?" She nodded her head and said, "Yes, but since you touched it, it is getting better." He held with both hands and soon her eyes brightened and she smiled and said, "The pain is gone."

This was the third miracle.

She wiped her tears and ran to her grandfather saying, "This monk makes magic!"

The grandfather said, "We are so grateful, the meal is on the house."

Dr. Usui enjoyed his breakfast and then the Fourth Miracle occurred. He had no indigestion, after breaking his fast with such a big meal.

He continued to walk the seventeen miles back to the monastery and arrived about dark. The young boy who opened the gate for him said, "Oh Dr. Usui! We are so glad you are back. We were just about to go looking for your bones."

Dr. Usui smiled at him and said, "I am glad to be back, and I have had success. Where is the Abbot?"

The boy said, "The Abbot has been down with arthritis and a backache for several days now. I will lay out your clothes while you bathe. The old monk will be happy you are home."

After he had eaten, he saw the Abbot who asked, "How was your meditation?"

"Success, success, success." replied Dr. Usui. He placed his hands on top of the futon covering the abbot as he told the old monk all about his meditation and vision. He was very excited as he told him that he had finally found that for which he had searched so many years.

The old monk then said, "The pain is all gone. My body feels good. I feel full of energy!"

Dr. Usui said, "This is Reiki."

Dr. Usui slept well that night.

Its Use

Now that his long search for Reiki was over, the next step was to deter-mine how to put it to its best use.

The next morning, the monks gathered to talk it over. They felt that the people who lived comfortably had the opportunity to see doctors, herbal-ists, or acupuncturists for help with their health problems. But for the poor, of whom there were a great many, there was no help. So, Dr. Usui decided to begin by treating the people in the vast slum. To meet the people, he would sell them vegetables. With a pole over his shoulder, he had a basket in front and a basket in back, both filled with fresh vegetables. He wore his tradi-tional monk's robe.

The first person he met asked, "Where do you think you are going?"

Dr. Usui responded, "I am going to sell vegetables to the people here."

"In those clothes?" the man said. So they exchanged clothes. Wearing a kimono made of patches, he was ready to meet the people.

Suddenly, he was surrounded by a group of teen-aged boys. After a game of harassment, they took him to the leader, the King of the Mendicants.

They took his vegetable baskets.

The King of Mendicants said, "I see a money belt under his clothes. Strip him!"

They took his kimono.

They took his money belt.

Then they asked him, "Why have you come into the slum if you have money?"

He told them about Reiki, that he had found the formula that enabled him to help others to be well.

He said, "The only thing I want, is to live with you, to have a place to practice this healing touch, a place to sleep, and a little food each day. But I will not go outside and beg. I will practice Reiki from sunrise to sunset, mak-ing people well."

They gave him dirty rags to wear, and provided him with a little food each day and a place to sleep and practice Reiki.

He chose young people for his first clients, because the cause in a young person is shallow. He only needed to work on them for one week. Older people have had their health problems longer, and it takes longer to bring them to a healing crisis. But then they get well quickly, like a new injury.

When each one had his/her health restored, Dr. Usui would say, "Go to the temple and ask for this monk. He will give you a new name and a job."

At the temples, they said that mind/spirit was most important, "why bother with the physical body... we have it such a short time, and we have doctors who take care of the physical ailments."

Dr. Usui had many experiences in the ensuing three years he spent in the slum.

One evening, as he walked around the slum, he saw familiar faces. He would ask, "Don't I know you?"

The person would reply, "Yes, Dr. Usui."

"Didn't I help you get well?"

"Yes."

"Didn't I send you to get a job?"

"Yes."

"Didn't you get the job?"

"Yes."

"Then what are you doing here now?"

"Oh, they wanted me to work from seven in the morning to seven in the evening. I worked for over a year, but it is easier to be a beggar."

Honest citizens worked long hours each day. These people did not appreciate being healed. They did not want to make changes in their lives. They placed the same value on his gift that they had paid for it... nothing.

He threw himself to the ground and wept.

The priests were right. SPIRIT COMES FIRST—THE PHYSICAL WILL FOLLOW.

He refused to treat beggars because of their lack of gratitude.

He returned to the monastery and talked with the old monk.

Then he devised the following creed to be taught along with counseling to find the cause of the ailment.

Just for today: Do not ANGER

Just for today: Do not WORRY

Just for today: COUNT YOUR BLESSINGS, honor your parents, teachers, and neighbors. Eat food with gratitude

Just for today: LIVE HONESTLY

Just for today: BE KIND TO ALL LIVING THINGS

The Pilgrimage

Dr. Usui decided to make a walking pilgrimage over all of Japan. When he would come to a place where many people were shopping, he would light a torch and walk through the town.

People who saw him would stop him and say, "Dear monk, this is broad daylight. You don't need a torch to see."

He would reply, "Dear people, I am looking for people who are healthy, happy and have enlightened hearts. There are some with sorrows, depression and physical pain who need to light up their life. Come to the temple at two o'clock and hear my lecture."

In this way, he found people he could help to restore their mental and physical health. He became known throughout Japan as a great healer. But he always acknowledged that it was not he who did the healing but God's Energy passing through him. He was only the vehicle being used for this purpose.

In time, Usui had eighteen masters teaching and practicing Reiki, and Reiki became known as a good alternative to the other forms of medicine.

Mikao Usui was decorated by the Emperor of Japan for his healing and teaching.

He was buried in a Zen Temple in Tokyo. There was a large tombstone on which is an engraving about his work for mankind.

Chujiro Hayashi described his master as a genius, a scholar and a philosopher. Mikao Usui had read, studied, and practiced the religious disciplines of Christianity and Buddhism for many more than the 27 years mentioned here, until he had reached a place in his spiritual growth where he was ready to accept in his heart the relationship of all living things to each other.

In the part of his meditation where he fell unconscious, holding the desire to be of service, with no thought of self-importance, no interest in material things and no ambitions of any kind, reaching out with unconditional love to help others to realize their own true Beingness, he moved into that Right Relationship with All That Is: that oneness with Pure Energy where he received his vision.

As he was coming back into the world of time and mind, he was given the pictures and sensations of understanding the symbols and ceremonies of Reiki as we know them and he was aware of "Remember, remember, remember."

The things most important to us, that he remembered, were these symbols and ceremonies because this is the way Reiki is brought to us, and the way we continue the teaching. But the most important thing to him was the remem-

Usui Sensei

brance of HOW TO RETURN TO THAT PLACE OF ONENESS WITH PURE LIGHT ENERGY. From that remembered place, all the lives he touched were changed.

He carried a lighted torch to attract attention so he could tell the people how to bring LIGHT into their lives. After his "lecture", when he had raised their consciousness (lightened their hearts) to the point where they could accept a change in their lives, Mikao Usui needed only to extend his hand to touch and feel the pulse of energy in order to restore their health. For good health is the "natural" state of our Being.

Isn't this the way that the great spiritual leaders have tried to show to the world?

Chujiro Hayashi

CHUJIRO HAYASHI was a commander in the Imperial Navy. He had learned English as the training ship he was on sailed to the major ports all over the world. He came from a family of well educated people who had considerable wealth and social status. He was forty five years old and in the Imperial Naval Reserve when he happened to be in a market place at the time that Dr. Usui came bearing his lighted torch and announcing his lecture at a nearby temple. The sincerity of this strange monk, as he talked about being able to bring about healing in other people, caught his imagination. The more he listened, the more intrigued he became with the concept and with the dedication of this monk as he walked all around Japan reaching out to help the depressed, the ill and the disabled.

Dr. Usui told him, "You are too young to retire. Come with me as I walk about to help people."

Hayashi respected Dr. Usui and believed in the good he was doing with Reiki, so he walked around the countryside of Japan with Dr.Usui, bringing healing to the ill and crippled people and teaching them how to heal themselves with Reiki; they were able to teach many young and old.

When Dr. Usui reached the time to make his transition, he asked Chujiro Hayashi to take the leadership of Reiki, to become the Master and teacher of the Usui Reiki System of Manual Healing. To be the one to find the new masters and to make certain that the Usui Shiki Ryoho, (Usui Universal Life Energy Art of Healing) continued as they had practiced it. Then Dr. Usui announced to all his followers that Hayashi was the one he had chosen to continue in his footsteps, and asked that they respect him and help him as they all continued to work to bring Reiki healing to all people.

Dr. Usui had talked to Hayashi about his experience at the beggars' camp, saying that with his face in the mud he began to think that he had made a great mistake.

1. First address the spirit.
2. Then heal the physical
3. Beggars lack a sense of gratitude.

Henceforth there shall be no more free treatments and no free classes. It takes a good mind and a good body to make a human being a complete whole.

The Reiki Clinic in Tokyo

Chujiro Hayashi opened a clinic near the Imperial Palace in Tokyo. It consisted of a reception room and a large room containing eight couches where sixteen practitioners could treat eight people. One practitioner worked on the client's head and the other practitioner sat on the client's right and worked on the stomach area, then both worked on the client's back. Treatments began at seven o'clock in the morning and continued until noon. There was an hour lunch break, and then the practitioners went out each one to make one house call, usually returning home by seven o'clock in the evening.

Someone aspiring to become a Reiki practitioner first had to be accepted by the masters in the Reiki organization, and second, had to promise to use Reiki daily and volunteer some hours to practice Reiki regularly at the Reiki Clinic.

Dr. Chujiro Hayashi never changed the System of Reiki, he simply brought it inside the clinic, with the practitioners still going out to the people who wished to be treated.

It appears that Chujiro Hayashi, as a military man, was more systematic than ascetic. He would logically be the one to organize the manner of teaching Reiki, beginning on the head with the four positions on the head, four positions on the front and four positions on the back as the basic treatment, adding other positions according to need. This is the way Takata was taught Reiki in Hayashi's Clinic. This is the way she taught her students.

Hayashi's Charity

Dr. Hayashi was always amused when Takata asked questions. Because it was so foreign to the ways of the Japanese ladies who never dared to question anything, he considered the direct wanting-to-know quality of curiosity which was so much a part of Takata as "American democracy in action."

As Takata was preparing to go back to Kauai to begin her practice of Reiki, she felt the need to have a question answered. In her year of working at the Reiki Clinic every day, she had observed that all the clients were well dressed, well spoken, and appeared to be people of considerable means and education. Some seemed to be very wealthy, well-known, and even royalty.

But what about the poor people? They had health problems, too. Why didn't they come to the Clinic? Were they being refused?

She found the opportunity and spoke to Dr. Hayashi, "In all these months that I have been here at the Reiki Clinic, I have never seen one poor person, nor anyone dressed shabbily or in rags. No laborers have come here. Is that because you refuse to treat poor people?"

Amused at her directness, Dr. Hayashi burst into laughter, saying, "You are always digging, digging, digging. But whenever you come out with a question it is because it has been working around in your mind and your curiosity has gotten the best of you. You ask about not seeing poor people here. I think your real question is, 'don't I do charity?'"

"When you become a practitioner and have a good deal of experience, you will encounter this situation, too. All these people who come here are above middle class. Whenever I am asked to do so, I go to the prince's house. They are intellectuals, well educated people from wealthy families. When they are ill, they go to the best hospitals, get the best doctor, and call in specialists. The surgeon will say that an operation is the quickest way to solve the problem. The internist will say, 'No, no operation. We don't believe in cutting this person.'"

"So when the doctors can't agree on the treatment for this patient, they call for Hayashi's Reiki. They are satisfied because it is a drugless non-invasive treatment. Results don't begin to show as quickly as with drugs, but on the fourth day they begin to see a difference. They begin to feel better and are vitalized. You see, we find the cause, and when the cause is removed, there shall be no effects. No illness, just good health, happiness, with the ability to take care of security and prepare for a long life. That's Reiki.

"You don't find raggedy people and poor people here because they do not accept Reiki. They go to the village doctor and they say he is very kind and tries to help them. But the poor don't accept him. They think they have to go to the big University Hospital and get a well-known medical professor to treat them and a nurse standing around them all the time and then they are going to get well. They are always dreaming and craving for things out of reach. They don't even bother to thank the village doctor for giving them treatment and medication. Their attitudes and understanding is different. They would not accept a drugless and bloodless treatment... they wouldn't accept me anyway.

"But if any person comes here for treatment, I never send them away. And when they call me, I don't care how poor, I'll go. Or I'll send a practitioner. Counting you, I have seventeen practitioners."

When she returned to Kauai she heard his words ring true. The local people didn't want to go to the plantation hospital because there was only one doctor. They preferred to go to Honolulu to the Queen's Hospital where there were fifty doctors. They never even gave the plantation doctor a chance.

And so she decided to leave Kauai.

Hayashi's Transition

One morning as Takata awakened, she sensed a presence. As she opened her eyes, she saw Dr. Hayashi standing at the foot of her bed, clad in a white silk kimono and a white silk skirt.

She thought, "This is a message. I must return to Japan at once." And the image standing before her faded away.

She took the next boat to Japan and went straight to the Hayashis' home. He greeted her and told her, "Rest from your trip for a few days and then go down to southern Japan where the spas are located. Work in the spas and learn all you can about the things they do to make a person feel better. I will send for you when it is time to come back here."

She worked and learned in the spas for three months, and then she received word to return to Tokyo.

When she entered the house she was aware of Dr. Hayashi pacing back and forth in a room. Back and forth. Back and forth.

Then he would open a chest, take out a uniform, look at it long and hard and then put it back in the chest and continue to pace back and forth in the room.

After three days, he made an announcement to the family. "There is going to be a great conflict, and as an officer in the Imperial Navy, I will be responsible for great loss of life. I have decided not to do that. Instead, I will make my transition next Tuesday at one o'clock. Please invite the family members and the Reiki masters."

He had a long talk with Hawayo. He told her that he had discussed it with the other masters and had decided that she was the one that he wanted to carry on his work. Mrs. Hayashi did not want the sole responsibility of keeping the clinic functioning as it had been. She felt it would be better to retire to their country house.

Takata was pleased to be given this honor. She thanked him for having so much faith in her and asked, "Give me ten years to get my girls established in life and then I will devote my life to Reiki."

He instructed her to leave Japan and return to her home, and told her in which places she would be safe during the war. He also told her what the outcome of the war would be. As with many people who practice Reiki, he had learned to trust the messages given to him through his own intuition.

On Tuesday, May 10 1940 they gathered and had a nice buffet lunch. While they were chatting with each other, Dr. Hayashi's tatami mat was brought forth and he came in dressed in white silk kimono and white silk skirt. He sat down on the mat and began giving his last messages to the people gathered there.

He said, "The procedure will be: first, one artery will rupture, then a second artery will rupture, and when the third artery ruptures, that will be the end."

He continued with his messages for those gathered around him, and would interrupt himself by saying, "The first artery just ruptured." Then later, "The second artery has ruptured." And finally began an incomplete sentence with, "The third... art..."—and fell over dead.

Lineage

In 1973, when Takata was 73, she stated:

Chujiro Hayashi became Mikao Usui's number one disciple and worked with Dr. Usui until he reached the time of his transition. Then Hayashi became the Master and Teacher of the USUI REIKI SYSTEM OF MANUAL HEALING. True to the method and tradition, it was respectfully fulfilled by Grand Master (O Sensei) Chujiro Hayashi until his transition in May 1941. And I, HAWAYO HIROMI TAKATA, was granted and willed to carry on this work in Japan and other parts of the world. At this time in 1941 there were only five living teachers, including Mrs. Chie Hayashi. Now they have retired with age and I am left with this great work for humanity... After thirty eight years of teaching and healing, I feel it is not enough. I would like to leave this wonderful Art, so necessary to all humans and all living beings; I would like to leave this Art with some young couple who would be dedicated to this work and to carry on.

She envisioned leaving her work to a couple who would bring youth and vigor to Reiki and carry on its traditions, but she did not find the "couple." Instead she initiated twenty-two masters, asking them to respect the leadership of her granddaughter, Phyllis Lei Furumoto, and giving them permission to make masters after her transition. She asked them to respect the sacred Reiki teachings and standards she had spent her life upholding.

4

Practicing Reiki

Takata's Teaching Lesson

In 1938, HAWAYO TAKATA was made a Reiki Master.

Her first request of Dr. Hayashi was that she be permitted to teach a class free for those people who had helped her so much during the long time of her grief over the loss of her husband and a sister, and her own physical pain and sorrow.

Dr. Hayashi admonished her, "Never teach a Reiki class free. For then, it has no value. The people will not value it enough to use it. You can return your gratitude to them by treating them when they need a treatment."

Dr. Hayashi and his daughter returned to Japan and Takata was accustomed to making her own decisions. She decided to give free lessons to her neighbors and her in-laws who had been so helpful to her in her need. She refused to have her two sisters in the class, saying, "I'll teach you later. I have to see the success of my neighbors first."

One day, she was hanging out her laundry when a neighbor came up to her and said, "My daughter is home from school today. She has a stomach ache. Please come treat her."

Takata replied, "You treat her. I taught you how to do Reiki so you could help your family."

The neighbor said, "It is easier to let you do it than to do it myself."

Another neighbor came to her one day and said, "Little Mary is home with the flu. Please come and give her a Reiki treatment!"

Takata said, "Didn't I teach you how to do Reiki? You do it!"

She replied, "I haven't tried to do it."

Takata went inside and hid and cried. "They have no gratitude! Forgive me Dr. Usui! Forgive me Dr. Hayashi!"

Her sister came and asked Takata, "Do you have time now to teach me?"

Her quick response was, "There is a fee!"

"Ooooh. How much?"

"Three hundred dollars. It doesn't have to be cash. You can pay me some each month."

She said, "I'll talk to my husband." When she told her husband, he said to her, "Did you ask her to teach you? If you asked her, you pay the fee. You take installments to her. You pay her twenty-five dollars a month."

She learned Reiki and paid in installments.

The first time her daughter had an asthma attack, she thought about the high price she had paid to learn Reiki and now did not have spare money for doctors, so she decided to treat the asthmatic child herself. Before she had finished the treatment, the child was breathing easily. IT WORKED!

She went to Takata and told her all about it. She said, "Now I know why you charged me so much. You wanted me to be a GOOD practitioner. I came to thank you."

Takata said, "Good. Now make good use of it."

Takata recalls, "She has used Reiki regularly and it has carried over into her business. She is also successful in business. It was the cheapest investment she ever made. She has gratitude. Those who had free lessons are not successful, even in business."

The Year That Was Most Difficult

1937 was the year that was most difficult for Takata. She said to herself, "My Goodness, with all of this trouble, trouble, trouble, here I am trying to do good and why do I have all these obstacles?" She would recall Hayashi's teachings, as he said "DO NOT ANGER." Later, she told us "I never flew off the handle, but I always said, 'Bless me God, You are the only witness and You know the truth and nobody else does. You help me, right?'"

"I meditated, and that was no fooling around. When I was alone in my room I meditated late at night and early in the morning, and then when I went to bed, I said 'Thank you for today's blessings. Thou art the greatest and Thou are the judge of all things.'"

So, the lectures were a success and Reiki was blessed in the newspapers and the stories told about all the complications arising.

After the Hayashis were well on their way back to Japan, the policeman paid Takata an unexpected visit and said to her, "You had a rough time, didn't you?"

She replied, "Well, because I am a country jack and I didn't know, but then you see I am always on the right, for when I came to Honolulu, country jack as I was, I got a license."

He asked, "Who gave you the license?"

She gave the name of the Japanese attorney who was the attorney for the county. She had gone to him and said, "I am from the country and I don't think about these things, but I am going to practice in Honolulu and I would like to have some kind of license. He said he was glad I had come to him and he gave me a license to massage and told me to frame it and put it in the room where everyone could see it."

The policeman then said to her, "I want you to be very honest. I'll bet you gave your teacher some presents, didn't you."

She said, "Sure, I gave him presents, why not? A guest comes from that far and you are going to send him home empty handed? No, I gave him presents and the police were eager to find out what they were. I gave him four one hundred pound bags of Hawaiian sugar. He likes oranges, so I gave him two cases of oranges. Everybody talks about Kona coffee, so I gave him some Kona coffee to take home. Then there were cases of pineapple, a Hawaiian product. And a case of ripe olives. And the people gave him koa bowls, a koa cane and lots and lots of leis.

"Then to the daughter I gave a brand new complete outfit for traveling and a dinner ring."

The policeman looked at her and stared and said, "What I want to know is how much?"

She said, "How much what?"

He said, "You know, how much?"

She told him in no uncertain terms, "If you are talking about how much money, my teacher in Japan is a very big man. He is not a poor man. He is first class, he has a large studio, he has a big home, and he has everything where very high class people live. He does not need money. He has money. Why would he come here and try to get even a penny out of a student just trying to get started in life. He comes here to give me moral support. To give me a lift and to start me on the right foot. Why would he want to take even a penny of it? No, no, you are wrong."

But then he said, "We had to investigate. We will not bother you any more because he is back in Japan and you have a license to practice Reiki."

She breathed a sigh of relief as she said, "I'm glad you know the truth. Even the newspapers have written the truth, and they have given very, very good reports about Reiki, Dr. Hayashi and everything that is connected with it."

Then the editor/owner of the Japanese newspaper came to her and said, "You have been embarrassed and you have been cheated and you have been blackmailed and harassed. I feel very sorry for you. You're a tiny woman and you have a very strong will and courage. Now let us sue these people, we have lots of witnesses, and let them stay behind bars for the good of the public. They are a damn nuisance to the public. You have a very good cause and a right to sue them."

She said, "Thank you. I wish to thank you very much for your kind support and help and for thinking about my welfare. Without friends like you, I could never have withstood this ordeal. Let me think about it."

LIVE HONESTLY

Jodo Mission

The editor of the local paper wanted Takata to sue shady Sadie, the lady who had caused her so much trouble. She asked to think about it before coming to a decision.

That evening, she talked with the Archbishop of the Jodo Mission. He was very interested in Reiki. He had lost his voice for seven years from laryngitis and had been forced into early retirement in Japan. His voice had been restored by three weeks of Reiki treatments given by Hayashi and Takata in Japan.

The church then gave him a new assignment which was to head the American division of the Jodo Mission in Hawaii. This included the west coast of California. Often, he would invite his good friend Takata to have lunch with him after services.

His first mission after arriving in Hawaii was to meet with the ministers and churches in Hawaii and then to meet with those in California. No one in this entourage of twelve could speak English. He said to Takata, "We do not speak English and when we go to the dining room we will not know how to order our food. We want you to join our entourage. Why not take a vacation with our ministers? Will you come with me and help us by translating?"

Takata said, "I am very honored. I think I need a little vacation from Hawaii. Thank you, I accept."

When she met with the newspaper editor she told him, "I am not going to sue Sadie. I am only a human being and who is to be a judge of another human being? That is to be left up to God. I came in peace, and I have been harassed, but that is one of the things that came across my path. I have to cross that road. It is all over now and I have won the case for your health and many others and I appreciate it. I go in peace and I stay in peace.

"The only way I can prove to the world that I am better is by improving myself. I will go with the Archbishop to the west coast of California, and after the tour, I will enter the National College of Drugless Physicians in Chicago. The money I would spend on lawyers' fees I will spend to educate myself, and when I return, I will be a better technician, a better therapist, a better practitioner. That's how I'm going to fight people, by improving myself.

"Thank you," she said, bowing low. "I will see you when I come back."

He stormed out muttering "Stupid fool."

Honolulu, 1939

Hawayo Takata finished her studies at the National College of Drugless Physicians in Chicago and returned to Honolulu full of confidence. Now she had a better understanding of the physical and technical aspects of the human body.

Her first thought was to pay a visit to the newspaper editor who had reported on the work Takata and Hayashi were doing. She wished to make amends because they had been in disagreement when she left to study in Chicago.

She greeted him with, "I am back, Mr. Editor, and I come to pay my respects to you."

He was all smiles as he said, "I think you did the right thing. You live by the ideals of Reiki. I thought you were very foolish to run away, but now you have come back with more credits to yourself. The money invested in your studies instead of lawyers' fees was invested well."

She started her practice by opening an office in Honolulu. One day she received a telephone call from the island of Hawaii. Two high school teachers spoke to her saying, "We saw your article in the newspaper and we are very interested. Will you take a short vacation and come and visit us? We want to hear from you all about Reiki."

Takata replied, "Thank you very much. I shall be there."

Mal de Mer

When the appointed time came for the trip to Hawaii, Takata bought a ticket for the boat trip from Honolulu to Hilo.

She boarded the boat and went down to her stateroom to leave her things before coming back on deck to wave good-bye. As she entered the room she heard moans and looked around to see a lady lying on the berth facing the wall, dressed in kimono, obi, haori coat and tabis. She was moaning and groaning in quite real discomfort. The ship was still tied up to the pier so there was very little movement. Sailing time was to be much later.

The very distressed voice groaned, "Whoever you are, I'm a very seasick woman. I haven't held a meal for three days and I'm very weak. I shall groan all night and disturb you, so please go find another room."

The boat hadn't even left the dock! And all rooms and even all the deck space was occupied. This was a pineapple boat carrying the students who were returning to Hawaii after working in the pineapple cannery all summer.

Without saying who she was, Takata went to her side and looked at her face. She saw a very miserable middle aged lady and she wanted to help her. Without saying a word she put her right hand between her kimono and obi over her stomach.

The lady groaned louder and then began to scream for help.

Between the screams, Takata realized she had made the most embarrassing mistake of her life. HER RIGHT HAND WAS ON THE LADY'S BILLFOLD. She was stuck. She must not remove her hand now. Her face was red and full of anxiety. She said, "Reiki, if your are with me...do your stuff in a hurry!" closed her eyes and concentrated on mental healing that the Great Cosmic Power should not fail.

In a minute her hand began to tingle. She felt the Reiki flowing through her hand and she knew the lady would stop yelling.

The lady did stop yelling, looked up into her face and with a smile said, "You gave me great relief! You just made magic! I apologize for making so much noise."

Takata took a deep breath, thanking the Great Energy for healing her so fast. It was like a miracle. Takata was very happy with the results and did not try to explain. She told the lady to lie still and rest while she went up on deck.

After saying good-bye to her friends on the dock, Takata went back below and found the lady calm and comfortable. She helped her undress, put her purse on the pillow, folded her haori coat and obi and put them away. Then she told her, "Now that you are in a more comfortable position I would like to help you some more so you can have a good supper."

She treated the lady for half an hour. Her gall bladder was working better, and the dizziness left after she treated her over the ears.

Now that her mind was clear, the lady apologized again for being so rude.

She ordered for the lady a light supper of plain soup and crackers, celery sticks, sliced apple and grapefruit. She could munch on these things without getting up. She enjoyed her first meal in three days. Takata told her to sleep well and upon their arrival in Hilo, she would awaken her in plenty of time to have a good breakfast before they docked. The next morning before arriving in Hilo, she awakened her roommate, helped her dress and together they went into the dining room where they enjoyed a hearty breakfast.

Her roommate peered through the porthole in the dining room and recognized her own family. She was eager to meet them and tell them how well she had survived the trip without sea sickness! She and Takata parted in haste. Each one had forgotten to introduce herself to the other. All the lady could say was, "Many, many thanks. That was the first trip I have been able to eat on the boat." She eagerly told the whole story to her family on the way home.

In later years, when she traveled on big ocean liners, Takata was able to help many sea-sick people; However, she always introduced herself first and explained the greatness of Reiki as strictly drugless, not faith healing—they did not have to believe—nor magic. It always worked for her and helped her make many friends. A little kindness and love go a long way.

Three people met her at the boat and took her to the little town of Pahoa. She stayed in the home of the town baker. She gave a two hour lecture about Reiki, followed by hot tea and cookies. This gave the people the opportunity to ask questions and to get acquainted.

It was midnight before she went to bed. THE MEETING WAS A SUCCESS! About a dozen people signed up for the class which would start at seven the next evening and continue for four nights.

A rumor pervaded the town and reached someone in the class about a young woman who had helped her sea-sick roommate, with full details of the story being passed around. Only thing was, they had forgotten to ask each other's names.

Pahoa

Most of the people in this village were homesteaders. They worked for the cane plantation or the sugar refinery, some were vegetable farmers and flower farmers, some raised chickens. There were acres and acres of orchids and anthuriums. A very interesting place, indeed.

Many people were curious about Reiki and with the recommendations of the first graduates, it became popular. The kindness and love that are a part of Reiki go a long way. The people in this village were a good example of it. Everybody wanted to invite Takata to tea or supper and they showered her with flowers and fruits.

One day, as she was having lunch, one of her Reiki students came running in. He said, "Mrs. Takata, did you help a seasick lady on the boat?"

She said, "Yes."

"Well, she is only a few doors away from here and she told us the story about the incident on the boat and that woman who made magic. Now we know it was Reiki you were using."

The mystery was solved. The lady taking Reiki called her friend to come and meet Takata. They had a big laugh over the stories and Takata apologized for frightening her by putting her hand over her wallet and she apologized for screaming.

That lady made a point of enrolling in the next Reiki class in Pahoa.

The second class followed in Pahoa and on the third day of that class, the grocer came in very excited. He had gone to feed his sow which had given birth to thirteen piglets the day before, and he saw that she had a high fever and was lying down in the pen. He had heard Takata say in her lecture that animals could be helped with Reiki, so he ran to fetch her to help him treat his sow.

She asked him to get two other friends who were in the class with him. They would all go as quickly as they could. They put the sow in the middle of the pen so all of them could get around her and covered her with wet gunny sacks. They gave her Reiki treatment behind the ears, front, and back, as best they could, for two hours. She must have liked it because she lay still without complaining and received the healing. Soon they heard her gently calling the piglets. They came running towards their mother, climbing all over her and eagerly suckling.

Their lunch was just a little late that day.

The owner of the pig came to class the next day wearing a big happy grin. He said that he had gained six times more than what he had paid for the Reiki class by saving the sow, not counting the little ones. This was a remarkable experience for Takata.

Some of the farmers experimented with day old chicks. They could treat them all at once by spreading their hands in the brooder for fifteen or twenty minutes. The weaker ones needed to be held in the hands for a few minutes. The chicks love it and peep gently.

For goldfish in a bowl, you can hold the bowl in your hands for ten minutes.

Flowers are interesting. Soak the stems of cut flowers in a bucket of water, snip the stem in the water and hold the stalks a few minutes. This will cause the water to rise towards the petals and the blooms will last.

Hold seeds in your Reiki palms for ten minutes before putting them into the ground.

In cultivating orchid seedlings, hold the jar with both hands a half hour every day. The results will be seen in a few days and comparison could be made between those and the ones without the treatment.

Reiki was so well received here on the big island! She really appreciated the enthusiasm and sincere effort to understand what Reiki was all about. Perhaps this was the place to establish a Reiki Health Center!

It all came about by October 7, 1939 which was within that same year. The large white house on Kilauea Avenue would be her Reiki Health Center in Hilo for ten years.

The House

One day, Takata received a telephone call from two school teachers on the big island, Hawaii, who had read in the Honolulu newspaper about Takata and the good that Reiki was doing, and had heard about her previous visit. They asked her to take a short vacation and come visit them so that they could find out what Reiki was all about.

One of the teachers met her when she arrived at the pier in Hilo. They were going to drive up to the volcano, about thirty miles from Hilo.

The teacher explained, "I have had eczema for seventeen years, and wherever there is an outlet, fluid oozes out. It is most unbecoming. I have tried all kinds of mineral baths and medicines, but nothing seems to give me relief. Maybe your method will help me."

Takata replied, "Thank you for asking me. I will do my best. We must find the root of your troubles. Find the cause, remove it, and there shall be no effect. As the treatment works, you become a complete whole."

As they drove towards the volcano, the teacher said, "I have to stop at this house for a few minutes to select my silk stockings. This old gentleman is a Real Silk salesman and he is at home today. I see his car."

As they drove into the yard they saw a sign:

THIS HOUSE AND LOT FOR SALE.

They found the old gentleman playing solitaire. After greetings, she made the introduction, "This is Mrs. Takata from Honolulu."

He was a bit hard of hearing and all he caught was the "Honolulu," and figured that she was interested in buying the house.

He looked up at Takata and smiled with tears welling in his eyes. He stood up, gathered the cards and threw them into the air. Looking up, he shouted, "HALLELUJAH! HALLELUJAH! HALLELUJAH! Finally it has happened. I am so happy!" And the tears rolled down his cheeks.

The teacher was so embarrassed she couldn't find words to say. So she poked Takata and said, "Say something."

What can one say in the face of so much jubilation? She took a deep breath and said, "Well, I had no idea I was going to buy real estate. I didn't bring a down payment."

He looked at her and said, "Who's talking about down payment? I didn't say I needed a down payment! All you have to pay me is sixty dollars a month. That's all I want for ten years. I am seventy two years old now and I have two sons in Honolulu who are asking me to come and live with them. I will have a room and board. The sixty dollars a month will give me pocket money and I will feel like a king. Please take this place over and come and live here."

Takata reasoned with herself, it is only sixty dollars a month. I can swing the deal. I'm gonna take it. The house is double walled, with four bedrooms, more like two stories, on an acre of land, well built with a half basement, a two car garage and maid's quarters in the back adjoining the garage. It is a very beautiful property. Perhaps I should move in right away. It is big enough for a Reiki Center. And I can bring my father and mother here. They will be very comfortable here.

She thought for a moment. She did not want to disappoint him... and the deal was like a dream. Her decision was quick, "I'll take it."

Instead of talking stockings they rode to the bank and drew up the papers for the sale.

She could always rent it if she decided not to move there. Her friend was more than pleased. Takata's head was full of future plans to renovate the house if she decided to move to Hilo.

The next day, she was admiring the area when a couple of people stopped by after they saw the FOR SALE sign was gone and asked her if she was the person who had bought the house.

Takata smiled and said, "Yes."

The people then warned her about her neighbor. They told her, "He has been unable to sell the house for many years, but since you are a stranger you bought it unknowing."

When Takata asked what was the problem the people would just say, "You'll soon find out. Good luck!"

She got in touch with a lumber yard, got some carpenters and began to make alterations and repairs. The people in Hilo were very kind and willing to help.

The head carpenter remarked one day, "Such a lovely home for you, Mrs. Takata, and the FOR SALE sign was here for three years. No takers and the local people weren't interested."

Uh oh. "Why? Did I buy this property blindly?"

He said, "Yes, because you were from Honolulu."

Now it comes. "Tell me, what are the defects?"

He said, "No there are no defects in the property, but it is the NEIGH-BOR."

She asked, "What about the neighbor?"

He said, "The neighbor is a widow with SIXTEEN children. Sometimes she can't control them. She has them all sizes including a set of twins. Most people simply cannot cope with that. So this house has been standing here with a FOR SALE sign until you came along without any intentions, and it just fell into your lap."

She figured a neighbor problem was no problem at all, and decided to go over and pay her respects. She didn't even know her name, so she introduced herself and said, "I'm going to be your new neighbor."

The lady was very charming as she said, "You must please excuse me. My children get pretty rowdy sometimes and I cannot control them. But they are only children and I have only sixteen."

Takata asked, "Why do you say ONLY sixteen? Isn't that enough?"

Her answer was, "Well, only three years ago I lost my husband. But if he had lived a longer life, perhaps I would have had twenty four! Two dozen! Who knows?"

They laughed together and Takata said, "You do have all sizes, don't you? Perhaps your older..."

"The oldest are 16 and 18."

"Then they will soon be out of school and if they are girls, soon be married. I am very happy that I am going to be your neighbor and I don't think it's going to be any problem."

The Neighbor

In a few weeks it was Thanksgiving, the house was repaired, ready to move in and settle down. She made a big bowl of potato salad, a chicken, and sushi (Japanese fancy cold stuffed rice balls. Very good.) She took a tray full along with her heart full of sincere good wishes for the holidays to the neighbor and said, "This is my first Thanksgiving here and I want to celebrate by sharing my happiness with you and your family."

The neighbor said, "The children will enjoy this. It will make our Thanksgiving a big one."

She asked the children to keep an eye on her new house so that no stray horses or cows would come in the yard and eat the flowers while she spent New Years on Kauai.

And so their relationship became very congenial and happy.

Absolutely no trouble with the family next door. When stray horses or cows would come into her yard, the children next door would come and chase them away. When her three mango trees were ready to harvest, the boys would come and help pick them. They would give Takata a bushel of the best. There was always plenty for all of them.

As time passed, they went to college. Some were married, and so there were sixteen no more. They had a beautiful relationship helping each other.

No problem at all.

Her First Center

This large white house was her first Reiki Center. She would settle here. The minute she began the alterations to be done on the house, she felt like she owned a great palace. She would listen to the rhythm of their hammers like music to her ears, and at night as she would go up to bed, she would touch the walls and say, "God, bless this house. This to me is a great Reiki Center. This is where people are coming with their troubles. And YOU are going to dissolve them and make the people well. So this is not only my house, but it is for the people who need help. I need your blessings." She would gently, very gently rub the walls from top to bottom as she walked up the stairs saying, "Thank you God, thank you God."

One day, after the supervisor left them, the three carpenters began really banging away at the nails. There was no rhythm to their work. It sounded like everyone was mad at the world. Takata spoke to them and asked, "Please stop pounding the walls and tell me why all this bang, bang without reason."

One of them spoke up and said, "Mrs. Takata, we are very happy working here. But today the supervisor came from another job and said that job should have been finished last month and the lady is very unhappy with the color of the paint. He told her we had painted the color of the sample she gave us and that to redo the job would cost her more money. She was furious and showered her anger on the supervisor. And so the supervisor came over here and shouted at us in anger and now we are banging away at your house. All of this was contagious. Please forgive us, Mrs. Takata. We didn't notice it but you are entirely different from other people. You have been very kind to us. When he comes back we will ask him not to bring any more of other people's troubles here to this home."

She telephoned the supervisor and asked him to kindly lay them off for the day and have them come back when they were in a better mood.

She explained to the workmen, "It may be my fault for buying a second-hand house, but to me this is my place and here I am starting a health center in the best way I know how. I pat my walls early in the morning and at night before going to bed, praying and meditating that this place will have peace of mind, lots of happiness and success. You are shattering all my good vibrations by pounding in anger and discontent!"

They listened to her and then said, "Sorry, we didn't know it was affecting you."

She continued to explain to them, "Houses, no matter how old, were once living pines or fir trees. They have changed their form but life still goes on and they have feelings, too."

When the supervisor came, Takata said to him, "I like your work very much. I am very happy that your work is advancing. But when you are unhappy, please do not come and pour that bad vibration into the workmen who then put bad vibrations into my walls. Please have them leave for today and come back another day to continue their work when they can whistle a tune of happiness. For today, let them leave now, for you are not happy and the workmen are not happy. To me, this house is just like a temple or a castle. I want to be a success. Whatever I do here, I will do with my heart and soul, for I bless the house and the walls every day and night as I meditate on all the halls and rooms. I say, 'Thank you God for blessings.' Please go home today."

The supervisor took off his hat and held it over his heart and said, "Mrs. Takata, this is the first time I have heard a sermon at work and this one was better than going to church. I will do as you wish."

She had a few words for him, too. "If you will apply this attitude to all your jobs, you shall be a great contractor."

Within a few years he became one of the most successful builders around Hilo.

When the renovations were complete, there were two rooms for treatments, a very large living room where people could sit and wait, a nice kitchen, an extended porch, and a screen porch where meals could be served, looking out on a beautiful yard.

She had a yard boy come part time to do a little more planting to beautify the place. In a few months there was a great transformation in the garden.

Before she had completed the alterations, people had begun to come for treatments. The two school teachers were the first and within two months their problems were cleared up.

The Ghostly Visit

Takata occasionally received messages from the subtle world. You have seen this from her descriptions of her meditation under the camphor tree and the voice saying Operation Not Necessary. After practicing Reiki, she became more open to the subtle world. The following story is best told in her own words.

"The next town we went to was Okala, another sugar plantation on the slopes of the mountain. My older daughter and I arrived at the village Japanese temple and were greeted kindly by the Reverend and his wife. She had been a classmate of my daughter at the girls' college in Tokyo.

"We went to bed fairly early after my Reiki lecture. We slept under a large green net out in the parlor. On the wall above was a loudly ticking clock which struck the hours and one gong for the half-hour. We were prepared with flashlights in case we needed to get up during the night.

"It was past midnight when we heard someone walking outside the net. There was a Japanese straw mat on the floor and the swishing sound was very clear.

"My daughter was first to speak. She said, 'Mother, do you hear what I hear?'"

"I said, 'Yes. Be quiet and see what happens.' She asked if she should put on the flashlight, and I said, 'No.'"

"It went around the net three times and the clock struck one gong. We still listened but nothing was said. So I said, 'Whoever you may be, if you wish to say anything, I am awake and ready to listen to you. Do you want to pass on a message?'"

"No answer. We waited and waited. The clock stopped ticking and everything seemed so quiet. We lay real still and tried to go back to sleep but it was impossible for a very long time.

"About seven o'clock in the morning we heard the phone ring. The minister answered it. Since we heard their movements we woke up and joined them for breakfast. We saw that the clock on the wall had stopped at one twenty.

"After our morning greetings, I asked the reverend, 'When did you wind the clock?' He said, 'Yesterday. It is a seven day clock.' I told him that it had stopped at one-twenty and talked to him about the walking around.

"He said, 'You had an early phone call from Hilo radio station. You had better phone them right away.' So I did. It was my sister from Lihue, Kauai, who had been trying to get in touch with me. I called her and found out that my brother-in-law, Kenichi, had passed away early that morning.

"The Reverend said, 'The footsteps you heard were your brother-in-law's. Perhaps he was in a coma and going into transition when he came to say good-bye to you.'

"I told him about something that happened when I was in Kauai October 2, two months ago. I went to visit Kenichi when he was ill and in the hospital. He was suffering from ulcers of the stomach.

"It was to be determined whether or not to operate after the examination and X-rays scheduled for December 1, 1938. He was in the hospital at that time. That night the family gathered at supper. There were six of us. My sister lighted the altar with candles and incense paying her respects to Kenichi's parents who had long passed on. All of a sudden we heard a voice speaking clearly and quite pleasantly. 'NOT TO BE DISTURBED. I AM THE MOTHER OF KENICHI WHO IS IN THE HOSPITAL TONIGHT. QUITE WORRIED ABOUT HIS CONDITION. SO I HAD TO COME TO ADVISE YOU NOT TO OPERATE. HE WILL DIE IF HE GOES UNDER THE KNIFE. ASK HAWAYO TO TREAT HIM WITH REIKI AND SOON HE WILL GAIN HIS STRENGTH.'

"I was surprised that she knew about my treatments and I asked her if I was on the right road during these years. She said 'YES. I KNOW EVERYTHING WHICH GOES ON. FIRST I MUST THANK KENICHI'S WIFE FOR ATTENDING THE ALTAR WITH FRESH FLOWERS AND TEA OFFERINGS, MANY SWEETS AND FRUITS. SHE HAS PERFORMED HER DUTIES WELL AS A GOOD DAUGHTER-IN-LAW.'

"I said, 'Please, Mother, help Kenichi get well soon.' I stayed there fourteen days and Kenichi got well fast.

"The family conversed with her for about an hour. We asked her where she lived. What was it like. She knew all about the grandchildren. She especially commended me on my healing. I expressed my gratitude to her for the opportunity to converse with her and said that she should call upon us more often.

"She said 'I ONLY CAME TONIGHT BECAUSE HIS LIFE IS AT STAKE. YOU MAY NOT MAKE THE RIGHT DECISION, BUT I, HIS MOTHER, HAD TO COME AND GIVE YOU WARNING AND ADVICE.'

"We thanked her and with words of parting she was gone.

"The next day it was an easy decision. No operation. He was well in two weeks. He should have taken his mother's advice and not returned to work until after the new year. But he did not.

"He was completely recovered and became restless sitting around the house. He returned to work in December. On December 20 he stopped by the hospital and complained about his stomach. He was being operated on before the family found out about it."

He died during the night, the clock stopped, and Takata heard the walking around in her room.

Parker Ranch

The Parker ranch is the largest ranch on Hawaii. All the property from the top of the mountain down to the beach belongs to this ranch and there are many cowboys handling the cattle.

Teaching the cowboys how to treat cattle was a new experience for Takata. But she knew how to teach Reiki and so she taught Reiki to most of the hands on that ranch. They told her how they used Reiki in their work.

When a cow was about to drop a calf, the cowboys would bring her into a shed. They would stay with the cow and when the calf arrived they would wrap it in a warm blanket and give it Reiki. They never lost one newborn. It was a great credit to the ranch.

The cows that were not productive were given Reiki treatments by the cowboys the way you would give a treatment to a human being. They would treat the head and then the stomachs, the vital organs and the reproductive organs. After they were given these longer Reiki treatments they became productive.

On one occasion, one of the cowboys was cutting the grass with a gasoline lawn mower when it jammed. Without turning off the lawn mower, he reached down to remove the clod that was stuck. As it dislodged the blade began to turn full speed. He lost a finger.

In the Reiki class, he had been told that any acute injury heals quickly. He picked up the finger, replaced it and tied it up with his neckerchief. He held it for half an hour. Then he felt a beating or vibration going through and there was no more pain. Then there was no more numbness. He looked at the finger and it was in place. He bandaged it and didn't even look at it for three days. He treated the finger every moment he had a free hand. When he unwrapped the finger and showed it to Takata, there was not even a scar.

He said, "Now that this finger is all healed, we can laugh about it. Otherwise, I would be without a finger. I give the credit to Reiki."

Takata was delighted to hear of their successes because she knew that Reiki works on everything that has life, including animals, fowls, and plant life as well as human beings.

Baby With A Stye

One of the ladies who heard her lecture on Sunday expressed her interest in taking the class beginning on Monday and continuing through Friday.

She told Takata, "My son will be one year old this Friday. He was born with a stye on his eye. I stayed in the hospital a little longer thinking that the stye would go away. But when I left the hospital, the stye was still on his eye. I asked the doctor if the baby should stay in the hospital. But he said that since I had to feed the baby I should take him home with me and report back in a week or two when the stye goes away."

She got a calendar to mark the time of the condition. After one week at home, the stye moved to the other eye. The next week it moved back to the right eye, then back to the left eye. He had fifty-two styes in one year.

Takata asked, "What kind of temper does he have?" ·

The lady replied, "He is a cry baby, a very hard child to please. Very unhappy. If you promise to take away styes, I will learn it."

Takata's words were, "Well, I do not promise anything. I am not the one who is going to guarantee you, because I am also a human being telling this to a human being. What if you do not practice what I teach you? Who knows? You should have trust in God. Reiki is God power. Who are you and who am I to question God power. In a one year old baby it should work very fast. We will go to the cause. The stye is the effect. If you find and treat the cause there shall be no effect. The stye has to go."

Takata went home with the lady and watched as she fed the baby and gave him a bottle. Then she put him down for his nap. He was a very light sleeper and would awaken within two hours with a scream.

When she was certain the baby was well asleep, Takata went to his crib and began to treat him. She worked about ten minutes over his eyes, then around the forehead, the back of his ears and on to the front, his chest stomach, liver, pancreas and internal organs. He did not wake up when she turned him over, much to the surprise of his mother.

As she treated his back she said "This child's kidneys are not up to par. He has a little more acid and is a little more toxic than other babies. I am sure that when you make a small change in his diet he is going to get rid of all these toxins. You are going to need a lot of diapers."

She treated his kidneys for forty-five minutes. Then she went back into the kitchen where they waited for him to wake up. Soon Takata said, "Mama, I think your baby is up." Slowly they opened the door, expecting him to be screaming as he awakened. Instead, the baby was walking around his crib with a rubber duck in his hand, pounding it around the edge of the crib rail. He didn't even look up as they entered the room.

Takata told the mother to prepare his bath, clean clothes and lots of diapers. The smell was very bad.

The baby was smiling and happily playing. Even when she put him in the bath, he continued to play with his rubber duck. She dressed him and gave him his bottle with juice.

The next day the mother reported that the stye was shrinking. Takata gave him three treatments and the stye was gone. Her instructions to the mother were, "Now that you can do it, hold his stomach, his liver, his kidneys. Then the rectum. Go right up his legs to his lower organs. That will clean him out. He must have more juice than milk. Don't give food and liquid together. Give milk by itself. Then only food. The food will digest better because there is no fermentation."

That was the last stye he ever had.

Lump

Two of the eager students at her center in Hilo were a fifty-two year old lady and her sixty-two year old husband.

One day, they came to Takata and asked for a treatment for her. The lady said, "I am on my way home from seeing the doctor. I live about nine miles above you."

Takata asked, "What did the doctor tell you?"

She said, "The doctor said to prepare for an operation because the lump is quite large."

Takata responded with, "Is that so? Well, let me treat you and see what Reiki can do. Are there symptoms? Did you have pain?"

She said, "No. No pain, but I have a very poor appetite, sometimes a dull headache, and sometimes in the morning, I also have nausea."

Takata asked, "Do you throw up anything?"

"Yes," she answered, "My bile comes up very bitter and I feel groggy like I'm seasick. Sometimes I have to hold my sides to keep from staggering. This has been going on for some time now. I thought it was a good idea to see my doctor."

Takata was quiet, closed her eyes and concentrated on all of the front of the lady. When her concentration was focused below the navel she was aware of the very large lump. She told the lady, "Oh yes, the lump is quite large. I am sure you will not have to rush the surgery because it took a few months for the lump to grow to this size . Why don't you wait awhile before deciding about surgery."

The lady asked, "What do you think?"

Takata replied, "I would like for you to come back about four times. I am sure the nausea will go away and you will feel lighter. You will experience more vigor and more ease in your mind because I do not think an operation is going to be necessary. I have a hunch that this is going to end up as a very happy event."

The lady looked Takata squarely in the face and said, "What do you mean?"

Takata's answer was, "Well, perhaps you are going to have a baby."

With the mention of the word baby, she blushed right up to her ears and she said, "Oh, you know I'm fifty two years old. This is terrible. This is an awful moment. When I saw the doctor he said 'operation.' Then I came here and like a big joke you say 'happy event!'" She turned and rushed out to the car.

Takata dashed out after her saying, "I didn't hurt your feelings. Don't get mad. What is wrong?"

Her husband opened the car door for her and slammed it after she was seated, then he turned to Takata for an explanation. "My wife is furious. What did you tell her that upset her so much?"

Takata looked at him straight in the eye and told him what she had told the lady, finishing with "...she might have a happy event."

The lady glared at Takata who suggested to her, "Relax. You have a good husband. I know your youngest son is twenty-one."

Her husband said, "Keep the appointment for tomorrow, please." He blushed up to his ears and drove off.

The lady returned the next day for her treatment saying she had a good night, no nausea, no headache, and even had a good breakfast. She apologized for being angry, saying that she was so shocked by the news. She was told, "There are two things you cannot have: orange juice and milk. Put these two in your stomach and they will clash. The milk will curdle immediately and that will cause gas. This affects the gallbladder. As long as you come here I will tone up your gallbladder so that your bile will be better for digestion. Then there will be no more morning sickness. Since your husband has taken Reiki he can take over from here."

She had an easy pregnancy and she easily delivered her baby boy. When the little boy was five years old, she dressed him in a little sailor suit and hat, gave him a little basket with notebooks and pencils, and brought him to visit Takata. She said, "Mrs. Takata, tomorrow he starts kindergarten. I believe he is so bright that the teacher will have no problem with this child. He is a very happy child, good natured."

Takata was pleased that both mother and son were a picture of health. They lived in a small village in the country. The husband became known as one of the best Reiki practitioners in the area.

Childless Couples

There was a couple who had been married for eighteen years and were still without children. They had begun to wonder if they could ever have a family. She was forty-eight years old and her husband was in his fifties at the time they approached Takata to ask if Reiki could help.

Takata's reply was, "I am sure if your system is vitalized you are not too old. You say you both would like to have a family. The best thing is for both of you to come for treatment. Take the lessons so you can keep up the treatments."

They started the treatments and after three weeks they began to feel they were in better condition, more vitalized. The following year, they had a child.

When she went to the hospital to have her baby, she asked that her husband give her Reiki treatments daily in the hospital instead of buying her a present. She had a normal birth and a healthy baby girl. The Reiki treatments sped up the return of the organs in her body to normal.

This proud mother wanted to name her daughter "Bundle of Joy" and asked Takata to be her second Godmother. Takata replied, "I will be most honored. But think for a moment... when this child goes to kindergarten, how is she going to write 'my name is Bundle of Joy?' That is too long for her. Perhaps at home, you may call her Bundle of Joy, but treat her like any other being and give her a name so that when she goes to school, she will not have a hard time writing it." Together, they laughed about the incident. She grew up to be a very intelligent and healthy child with a name that was easy to spell and say.

Soon, other childless couples began to call on Takata. Some had been married eight or ten years. She always recommended that both people take Reiki classes so that each time they held the baby they would be giving the baby a treatment, saying, "This will keep the baby's vitality high and resistant to colds and contagious diseases."

At Christmas in 1948, Takata returned to Hilo to spend the holidays with family and friends she had left behind when she moved back to Honolulu.

One young woman came to her and said, "We have been married nine years and we want a family, so we plan to adopt a child."

Takata asked, "How far have you gone with the adoption?"

She replied, "We have signed papers with a doctor so they will call us for the first unwanted Oriental child born at the hospital."

Takata told her, "If you are sincerely thinking about this, why don't you talk it over with your husband and come to me for treatments. Many others had done this, and they do Reiki and they have children. When you decide, come and see me."

The next day, there was a knock at the door. Takata opened the door to find the young lady standing there with suitcase in hand. She invited her in saying, "I think you should stay three weeks. I'll give you a little change in diet and daily treatments. This will make your body more alkaline. A baby will not form if the system is too acid. You will be able to have your baby this year."

The Reiki treatments began early in February, and in the last week of November she gave birth to a bouncing baby boy. He was very alert and healthy. They were delighted to have their own baby instead of adopting.

Five years later, the young lady returned to Takata saying, "This time we want a little girl. We are very happy to have our boy but we think he needs a companion." When she went back home she had another baby boy. They felt their family was then complete.

There was a lady in a hospital who wanted very badly to have a child but she had miscarried three times. Takata advised her to begin having Reiki treatments before she became pregnant. She did that, and the next time she was pregnant and felt like she might miscarry, she went to the hospital and had someone call Takata. With daily treatments and help from Takata, she was able to stop the miscarriage and to carry through to term.

She had twins.

The Funeral

Takata was sweeping her sidewalk early one morning in 1938, preparing for the day's appointments, when her neighbor's brother drove up in a car. He had come to pick up his sister and drive over an hour away to their parents' home. Their mother had just passed away and they needed to consult about funeral arrangements.

As his sister came out to join him, she came over to Takata and with tears in her eyes said, "Mrs. Takata, I have come to ask a great favor of you. I have word my mother passed away this morning at five o'clock and my brother has come to take me home. This has been a very great shock because I did not think she was so sick. She had the flu and a fever but it didn't seem serious. So I am conscience-stricken to think that I was neglectful. If you would go with me for moral support, perhaps I will have the strength to face this sorrow."

Takata said, "Of course, if it will make you feel better."

During the long drive, this sister cried in remorse for her lack of concern and regret that she had not done more for her mother.

Takata asked, "Why are you so desperately sad about your mother's transition? She is sixty-two years old. That's a natural life span for many people."

The brother said, "We have been careless and ungrateful to her. I was away on the Mainland for seven years and I didn't do much to give her happiness. I came back recently but I haven't been able to do enough to repay her for her great love and the material help she gave me."

The sister said, "I live in Honolulu, but I have been too busy with my own business and my own life. I feel I have neglected her. And now it is too late. I'm so sad. I can't stop my regret and tears."

Takata, sitting in the back seat, was petitioning God, "If You have ears, please hear them, for only You can do anything about it."

When they arrived at the house, they saw many neighbors helping to prepare for the funeral. Men in white shirts and black ties and black pants were carrying the black cloth covered coffin into the house. Some people were making traditional white paper flowers. Some ladies were working in the kitchen.

Takata and the sister went into her mother's bedroom, where she fell on her knees, crying, and calling to her mother in Japanese, "Oka San, forgive me for being too late."

Since she had never met this family, Takata felt out of place and decided the best thing to do would be to stay out of their way. It was a new experience for Takata to be asked to come where a person had passed on and had no life. She could think of nothing to do or say to console them, so she got a low stool and sat by the body of the mother. Not knowing what else to do, she placed her hands on the solar plexus of the corpse.

It was now nine o'clock in the morning. The mother had been declared dead for four hours.

On the wall was the doctor's death certificate to permit burial.

Takata worked over all the inner organs, with one hand over the heart for over an hour.

About ten thirty. Taktata began to feel a little warmth around her navel... or was it just imagination?

She kept her hands on the body and prayed harder.

All of a sudden, the old lady opened her eyes and gave a long sigh.

Unbelieving, and still holding her hands on the solar plexus, Takata stood up and looked into the lady's eyes. When she saw her blink she softly asked, "Are you awake?"

After another long sigh, the reply came, "Oh yes. I can see you."

Takata sat down again and nudged the daughter who was crying inconsolably. "Stop crying. Wipe your tears. Very gently and quietly come around to the other side of the bed. Your mother is asleep no more. She is alive and awake."

The daughter yelled into her ears, "Oka San!"

Soon they heard the woman whisper, "I heard someone calling. I almost went through that little hole in the tunnel. I just caught myself in time. I heard you calling, so I came back."

Sister quietly called her father who ran to his wife's bedside.

The recently deceased lady sat up and said, "I'm hungry. I'd like to have some saimin (noodles)."

Before he could leave the room to prepare the saimin, Takata motioned to him and looked up at the burial certificate hanging on the wall. He side stepped like a crab, quietly removed the paper and slipped it into his pocket so she would not see it.

Takata treated her for another hour, still astounded at the power of God.

The father went back into the living room and quietly asked the men to carry the coffin and the flowers out the back door, away from the house and burn it. IT WOULD NOT BE NEEDED! He asked the people to leave quietly, one by one.

Takata returned to treat the lady another two days as she became stronger and able to eat more. Her son took Reiki and treated her daily. They remembered what they had said in grief and were so happy to have the opportunity to do something for their mother. They set about planning for it and in six months their parents were able to take a trip back to Japan, laden with gifts of pineapple, chocolate, coffee and sugar for their friends.

WHAT A GREAT JOY AND HAPPINESS!

Takata said, "In Reiki we do not lose hope. Where there is a spark of life, we work harder and ask God for blessings."

As she concluded her treatments, Takata asked the mother, "When you were in the deep sleep, where were you? Do you remember what you experienced?"

She answered, "I remember clearly. When I lost my consciousness, I was in a different sphere where I was being transported very swiftly through the air. I had no feelings, no aches nor pains. I saw a tunnel which had a large entrance. When I went through the entrance I discovered it was a very long tunnel with a light at the far end. That opening was so small that I wondered how I could go through it, but I knew that if I did go through it I would never return. I tried to decide whether I should go through or hold back. At that time I heard my daughter's voice calling me, 'Mama, Mama.' She was so unhappy and suffering so deeply that I came back. It was such a long, long sleep that when I awakened, the first thing I noticed was my hunger."

The amazing thing about her recovery was that it was total and perfect. She was mentally clear, her brain was not damaged. Reiki vitalized her. She had no fever, no aches, no pain.

After they had enjoyed a trip to Japan for six months, they returned to Kauai. This lady was enterprising. She already had a store. She added a saimin stand and a little soda fountain. Then she bought a nice place of business for her son. She was able to live fully and actively for the rest of her life.

5

A Personal Perspective from Fran Brown

Reiki's Spiritual Teachings

Each initiation fills each person with all the Reiki Energy that the body can hold. And so they must take place on different days in order that there be room for that body to contain more of the energy. Have you ever been so filled with unconditional loving light energy that you thought you might explode or something? Initiates experience many different sensations at that time. And that is the main reason that Reiki classes are held for several hours each on at least three different days. The other reason is that it takes time to integrate the message being presented, even though learning may come easily and quickly to those who come to class.

Very deep spiritual, emotional, and physical changes are instigated by the initiations. The body needs time to adjust to these changes. One does not easily comprehend the depth and power that is produced at these times. Only after the initiate has given daily treatment for some time, can this be realized. This is the reason that Dr. Hayashi required each initiate to work in the Reiki Clinic at least a few hours each week for many months after taking the class.

Today, we hear much said about living one day at a time. Dr. Usui was admonishing people to "be here now" over a hundred years ago. For Now is the only time there is. Whatever the challenge may be, put your best effort into dealing with the situation as it is right now. If you can handle the opportunities and the responsibilities you meet today, you can also handle the ones that will come to you tomorrow. The ones you did or did not handle yesterday are past, gone,—give no energy to them. Put your energy into the events of today.

When one has practiced living in the Now and has discovered the success it brings, perhaps it is time to attempt to come to terms with one of the precepts.

Any of the suitable current methods can be used to separate the Self from the emotionalities, by realizing the Self is what we Are, and the emotionality is a condition to be involved in by choice. By becoming involved in ANGER, there is no choice of action—only reaction—meaning that the person or action pushing the ANGER button has all the power.

A thought-provoking question might be: if a person is using his/her energy to push buttons, is she/he going to make good use of the additional energy given away by the one angered? Occasionally, a good purpose is served by choosing to give away energy in anger. Usually, that is not the case and only discomforts are generated.

When living is one day at a time, much of the stress has disappeared. A higher degree of comfort is reached without the contention of anger.

WORRY is the next one to release one day at a time. And with the knowledge that since the best effort has been put forth at the time of the action it really doesn't matter what the outcome is.

One person said, "It pays to worry. All the things I ever worried about never came to pass."

This is usually true, only peace of mind has been sacrificed. How much better to sleep soundly with peaceful rest.

Many pages have been written about maintaining an ATTITUDE OF GRATITUDE. Writing a list of all the desirable things coming to mind in ten minutes can be astounding. A daily practice of listing these things can open the mind to the abundance of good things all around. It becomes easy to see there is success and plenty for all needs, but not greeds. Thus develops a consciousness of abundance to replace a poverty consciousness, the feeling of not enough.

HONOR and respect the Divine, the Creative Energy, the unconditional love that is the center of all that has life, even though it may be successfully hidden from view—it is there, in all— allow each its own Beingness. Parents, teachers, (even button pushers are teachers), neighbors, others; all living things deserve to be honored.

LIVING HONESTLY can bring a startling self-awareness. To spend a whole day observing each choice and action in the light of honesty can be very trying, even inconvenient. It means stopping at all the stop signs even when nobody is in sight. Honesty lives inside and cares not about being placed where others can view it.

Practicing Reiki every day and holding thoughts like these, the practitioner will find new worlds opening, new talents emerging, successes at hand, and an abounding unconditional love for all life. The heart becomes lighter as it is continually filled with the light of unconditional love. Limits contrived by daily habits tend to disappear. Needs are met, the unneeded falls away. The life of the practitioner changes, becomes clearer and simpler.

Mikao Usui called it THE LIGHT RESEARCH ASSOCIATION. One translation of the character for LIGHT is INNER LIGHT.

His interest was in bringing the light of spiritual growth, raising the consciousness of the people, helping them to be aware of their own Divinity and that of all life around them. The moment a person realizes this, healing of the body occurs. Anyone holding this realization can place a desire in mind and watch that thought materialize, e.g. the spoon you are holding slowly bends downward as though it were made of warm wax.

Reactions

Each time Takata taught a class she would talk about "reactions."

When Reiki treatments are begun, a great change takes place, and all the energy bodies are affected as the physical body begins to detoxify itself. The cleansing of the physical body starts as the vitalized organs begin to return to normal. This is called "reaction," and after this is finished, the body is much more normal and is then able to heal itself. The reaction shows whether the healing is moving forward.

Things long forgotten may surface, stirring up much emotion. That is the time to deal with them, to forgive the situation and release them.

Spiritual growth accelerates as new ideas come forth, and things no longer needed drop away. Even the choice of which friends to spend time with seems to change.

With this introspection, self-awareness grows and subtle gifts manifest, bringing to light new talents. Healing takes place on many levels.

The Turquoise Earrings

One day when Hawayo Takata was a guest in my home, we were sitting at dinner and she removed her turquoise earrings and passed them around. She asked us to observe them carefully and tell her what we saw. As we looked them over she told us a story. She said these turquoise earrings, with stones about the size of a dime and mounted in silver, were her favorites. They were small enough for her and they looked nice with her tumbled turquoise necklace.

That year it was the fashion to wear turquoise jewelry mounted in gold and she decided to have her favorite earrings mounted in gold instead of the silver settings. She took them to a local jeweler in Honolulu and asked, "Will you please change these earrings for me? I want them mounted in gold."

He replied, "Bring them back in February and I will do it for you. Right now is the Christmas rush. After Christmas I will have time to do it.

She looked forward with great anticipation to wearing her new golden turquoise earrings. In February she took them to him again. This time he looked at them carefully and said, "You don't need to have them remounted into gold. They are already set in gold."

With that remark, the people listening to the story looked very closely again at the earrings. All agreed that the metal surrounding the turquoise stone was shining yellow and heavy. Only the clip looked like pot metal. The turquoise stone had several matrix lines in it, as does all turquoise.

Several years later when she was visiting again, the same earrings were passed around with the same observations following the same story. Only this time, we could see that the clip that touched her ear was a shiny yellow and the lines of matrix in the turquoise had disappeared and the stone was now a clear blue.

The Ring

January of 1979 was very cold and the mid-west was deep in snow. Takata and I were snowbound in her home for a week while she was training me to be a Reiki Master. Several weeks later we were scheduled to teach a Reiki class in Phoenix. Team teaching was Takata's way of helping a new master develop into a seasoned teacher. Takata welcomed the opportunity to get out of all that snow and team teach a class where it was warm.

When she arrived at the hotel where the class was to be held, she took off a ring she was wearing and asked me, "What color is this ring?"

Upon close observation of the plain little band with some markings on the outer surface, I thought it looked like a white metal, not quite like sterling silver. When I asked if this were her wedding ring, she replied, "Oh no, this is a cheap little ring I bought at a temple for a dollar or two."

Wednesday was the lecture for anyone who wanted to know about Reiki. Thursday, Friday, Saturday and Sunday were the classes. She said they were supposed to last two hours a day, but she had so much to tell and so much to teach that they always lasted four hours each day.

At the end of the last session, on Sunday, she took off her ring and passed it around for all to see. She said, "Look at it closely and tell me what you see."

Everyone said "A plain gold ring with a little design around it."

When it came to me it was a shock for me to feel the weight of it and see the yellow shine on the ring she had shown me days before and had been wearing every day as she prepared our meals, went about her personal business, and taught the class.

Takata was honest in her teaching and in her dealings with people. Live Honestly is one of the Reiki principles and she truly lived Reiki. It would have been out of character for her to trick me. I felt she was simply sharing a phenomenon that she had discovered could happen.

For many years now, my studies have told me that the mind has far more capability than we humans realize or know how to use. Discovering new ways to use this valuable tool ads excitement to daily living. IF YOU CAN DO IT, I CAN DO IT is central to these teachings.

With this in mind I began to wear a silver ring with the intention of seeing it turn to gold. A week later that ring was still silver. Perhaps another twenty years of practicing Reiki, daily meditation and prayers will lead to that state of self awareness which will see such phenomena happen. But I know they only happen when there is no ego involvement and is not important to the practitioner. Turning things to gold is NOT what Reiki is about. Nor is it about any of the things that give status, riches or glory to the practitioner. These attitudes IMPEDE the workings of Reiki.

REIKI IS UNCONDITIONAL LOVE and when offered from one person to another, healings can occur. Takata taught us to invoke the Reiki energy, to pay attention and give a good treatment, then to RELEASE IT TO GOD. Leave it to God HOW the healing will come about. In other words, don't tell God how to run his business.

Conversations With Takata

In the seven years that I knew Hawayo Takata, we had numerous occasions to talk about Reiki, its practice and its intent.

Hawayo Takata devoted her life to Reiki and more specifically, to the Usui System of Natural Healing. In the Japanese language, Reiki means "spirit," which is to say the Universal Life Force, an energy living through each of us. The specific method or "initiation" for instilling this "system" of promoting healing in another was given to Usui in his vision. He charged Hayashi, who charged Takata, to keep this system intact.

She taught us to treat Reiki with the respect it deserves. The information transmitted is sacred. She urged us to treat it with due respect and do nothing to diminish it. To learn Reiki cost her dearly in 1936-1938, and she exacted a promise from her masters that those costs remain the same even though the cost of living has risen dramatically.

Hayashi taught Takata to do the treatment with a specific sequence and manner of placement of hands, beginning with the head, treating down the front, then the back and ending by treating specific places of problems. She practiced this method daily in the company of other practitioners for a year and found that her intuition was giving her more and more information. She continued to practice Usui's System as a prevention and told us to listen to our intuition.

She continually gave thanks to God for all she received and was diligent in her daily prayers and meditations, affirming that "It is not I that does the healing, but the God Power coming through me that heals." She told me to place my hands as I was taught, to trust my hands, and allow the Reiki Energy to flow through me into the fully clothed client without concerning myself as to how or when the healing would take place.

She stressed the need for humility because the ego's desire for power and recognition creates a block to healing. During the time of teaching, she would not permit even one small glass of wine with dinner, insisting that Reiki Energy was not to be mixed with any other energy. There are many paths back to the Source. They all work when their protocol is followed. Reiki is one path and it is not to be mixed with another even though they may feel compatible.

Today and Tomorrow

On December 12, 1980, Hawayo K. Takata, made her transition. After a year, her Reiki Masters met, many for the first time, for a week together in Hawaii. At the end of our meeting a memorial was held at the Buddhist Church in Hilo where her ashes are interred.

She left us a magnificent gift—Reiki—and the hope that we would take good care of it, as she had, and make it available to all the world.

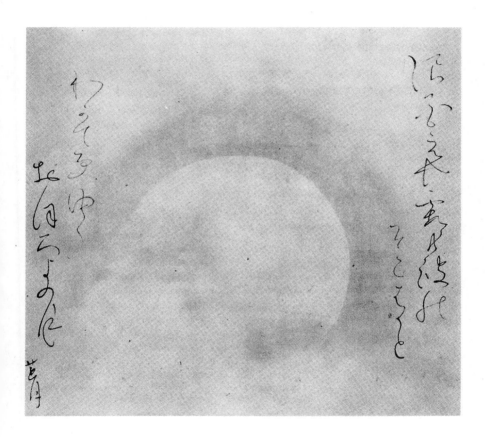

Reiki produces good health, happiness and security

Just for today, do not worry

Just for today, do not anger

Honor your parents, teachers & elders

Earn your living honestly

Show gratitude to everything

Dr. Mikao Usui

When these rules are applied daily, the body will respond and whatever we wish to attain will be within reach.

Takata taught us to "live Reiki:" a comfortable, joyful and gentle life of good Health, Happiness and the Longevity we all seek.

Takata Made These Students Masters

George Araki
Dorothy Baba
Ursula Baylow
Rick Bockner
Patricia Bowling
Barbara Brown
Fran Brown
Phyllis Furumoto
Beth Gray
John Gray
Iris Ishikuro
Harry Kuboi
Ethel Lombardi
Barbara McCullough
Mary McFadyen
Paul Mitchell
Bethel Phaigh
Shinobu Saito
Virginia Samdahl
Wanja Twan
Barbara Weber Ray
Kay Yamashita

FRAN BROWN has lived most of her life in the San Francisco Bay Area, where she married, raised three sons and was widowed. In 1972, she began a spiritual search that led her into an awareness of her own healing gifts. She met Takata in San Francisco in 1973 and became Takata's 7th Reiki Master in January, 1979. She has devoted her life to teaching Reiki, travelling all over the world, wherever people want to learn.

Fran writes: *To be a teaching master is my way—but it is not the goal of most Reiki practitioners, nor should it be. There is much need in this world for those who can help change the direction of a person's life and guide it into productive good health. There are many practitioners who today are facilitating the kinds of healings mentioned in this book. Many of them may be experiencing phenomena similar to that described in the stories. All of them certainly are finding their spiritual growth accelerating as they practice Reiki. Reiki Centers are being established in many places in the world, so that this gentle offering of unconditional love can reach all who search for it.*

LIFERHYTHM PUBLICATIONS

Bodo Baginski & Shalila Sharamon   **REIKI**   Universal Life Energy
200 pages   illustrations
This was the first book ever written about Reiki and it became a runaway best seller. With the help of specific methods, anyone can learn to awaken and activate this universal life energy so that healing and harmonizing energy flows through the hands. Reiki is healing energy in the truest sense of the word, leading to greater individual harmony and attunement to the basic forces of the universe. This book features a unique compilation and interpretation, from the author's experience, of over 200 psychosomatic symptoms and diseases

Müller&Günther   **A COMPLETE BOOK OF REIKI HEALING**
Heal Yourself, Others, and the World Around You
192 pages, 85 photographs and illustrations
This book includes the history and practice of Reiki, with photographs and drawings as well as clear instructions for placement of hands in giving Reiki. Brigitte Müller was the first Reiki Master in Europe and she writes about her opening into a new world of healing with the freshness of discovery. Horst Günther experienced Reiki at one of Brigitte's first workshops in Germany, and it changed the course of his life. They share a vision of Reiki to help us all heal ourselves and our world.

John C. Pierrakos M.D   **CORE ENERGETICS**
Developing the Capacity to Love and Heal
With 16 pages of four-color illustrations of human auras corresponding to their character structure, 300 pages
John C. Pierrakos, M.D., is a psychiatrist, body-therapist and an authority on consciousness and human energy fields. The focus of his work is to open the "Core" of his patients to a new awareness of how body, emotions, mind , will and spirituality form a unit. Dr. Pierrakos is considered one of the founders of a whole new movement in therapeutic work, integrating body, mind and spirit and this book has become classic.

John C. Pierrakos M.D.   **EROS, LOVE & SEXUALITY**
The Unifying Forces of Life and Relationship
150 pages
The free flow of the three great forces of life—eros, love and sexuality—is our greatest source of pleasure. These three forces are simply different aspects of the life force, and when we stay open, they are experienced as one. They generate all activity, all creativity. This book has been long awaited. John Pierrakos, the great psychiatrist, was a student and colleague of Wilhelm Reich, and co-founder of Bioenergetics; he later developed his own therapeutic work, Core Energetics.

Anna Halprin   **DANCE AS A HEALING ART**
Returning to Health Through Movement & Imagery
195 pages   illustrations
In this graceful book Anna Halprin offers the wisdom of her life experience as a dancer, teacher and healer. As a cancer survivor, she tells her own story and that of many others with deep compassion and uplifting clarity. Originally written as a manual for teachers, this book is filled with guidance and insights into the emotional processes of a health crisis— as well as clear guidelines for leading groups and classes in healing movement

Malcolm Brown, Ph.D. **THE HEALING TOUCH**
An Introduction to Organismic Psychotherapy
320 pages 38 illustrations

A moving and meticulous account of Malcolm Brown's journey from Rogerian-style verbal psychotherapist to gifted body psychotherapist. Dr. Brown developed his own art and science of body psychotherapy with the purpose of re-activating the natural mental/spiritual polarities of the embodied soul and transcendental psyche. Using powerful case histories as examples, Brown describes in theory and practice the development of his work; the techniques to awaken the energy flow and its integration with the main Being centers: Eros, Logos, the Spiritual Warrior and the Hara.

Ron Kurtz **BODY-CENTERED PSYCHOTHERAPY: THE HAKOMI METHOD**
The Integrated Use of Mindfulness, Nonviolence & the Body
220 pages, illustrations, $15.95

Hakomi is a Hopi Indian word which means "How do you stand in relation to these many realms?" A more modern translation is "Who are you?" Hakomi was developed by Ron Kurtz, co-author of The Body Reveals. Some of the origins of Hakomi stem from Buddhism and Taoism, especially concepts like gentleness, compassion, mindfulness and going with the grain. Other influences come from general systems theory, which incorporates the idea of respect for the wisdom of each individual as a living organic system that spontaneously organizes matter and energy and selects from the environment what it needs in a way that maintains its goals, programs and identity. Hakomi is really a synthesis of philosophies, techniques and approaches that has its own unique artistry, form and organic process.

Helmut G. Sieczka **CHAKRA BREATHING**
A Pathway to Energy and Harmony
100 pages Illustrations

A guide to self-healing, this book is meant to help activate and harmonize the energy centers of the subtle body. The breath is the bridge between body and soul. In today's world as our lives are determined by stressful careers and peak performance, the silent and meditative moments have become more vital. Remembering our true selves, our natural energy balances are restored. Chakra-breathing enhances this kind of awareness and transformational work, especially on the emotional and energetic level. *Supplemental Cassette Tape of Guided Meditations Also Available*

R. Stamboliev **THE ENERGETICS OF VOICE DIALOGUE**
Exploring the Energetics of Transformational Psychology
100 pages

Voice Dialogue is a therapeutic technique based on the transformational model of consciousness. This book approaches the human psyche as a synthesis of experience-patterns which may be modified only when the original pattern of an experience has been touched, understood and felt from an adult, integrated perspective, developing an "Aware Ego". This book explores the energetic aspects of the relationship between client and therapist, offering exercises for developing energetic skills and giving case histories to illustrate these skills. Voice Dialogue is the work of Hal and Sidra Stone Ph.Ds.

Allan Sachs D.C.   **THE AUTHORITATIVE GUIDE TO GRAPEFRUIT SEED EXTRACT**
A Breakthrough in Alternative Treatment for Colds, Infections, Candida, Allergies, Herpes, Parasites & Many Other Ailments

Dr. Allan Sachs' revolutionary work in treating Candida albicans imbalance, food allergies and environmental illness has inspired thousands of patients and a generation of like-minded physicians. Based on his training as a medical researcher and his lifelong interest in plants, he undertook an intense study of the antimicrobial aspects of certain plant derivatives, expecially grapefruit seeds This is a complete hand book, giving information on the therapeutic use of grapefruit seed extract and its use for many house hold, farming, and industrial needs as well as for treating animals.

R. Flatischler   **THE FORGOTTEN POWER OF RHYTHM TA KE TI NA**

160 pages, illustrations

Rhythm is the central power of our lives; it connects us all. There is a powerful source of rhythmic knowledge in every human being. Reinhard Flatischler presents his brilliant approach to rhythm is this book, for both the layman and the professional musician. TA KE TI NA offers an experience of the interaction of pulse, breath, voice, walking and clapping which awakens our inherent rhythm in the most direct way—through the body. It provides a new understanding of the many musical voices of our world. *Supplemental CD Also Available*

Cousto   **THE COSMIC OCTAVE**   Origin of Harmony

128 pages, 45 illustrations, numerous tables

Cousto demonstrates the direct relationship of astronomical data, such as the frequency of planetary orbits, to ancient and modern measuring systems, the human body, music and medicine. This book is compelling reading for all who wonder if a universal law of harmony does exist behind the apparent chaos of life. Tuning forks, tuned to the planets, earth, sun and moon, according to Cousto's calculatlions are also available.

LifeRhythm
Books for Life Changes

P.O. Box 806   Mendocino CA 95460   USA
Tel: (707) 937-1825   Fax: (707) 937-3052
http://www.LifeRhythm.com
email: books@LifeRhythm.com